CW01658892

DED

This book and these memories are dedicated with much love to my children: Samantha, Melissa, Natasha and Davina; my grandchildren: Emma, Jake and Zach; and my ex-wife, Sherry.

PREFACE

The covid pandemic changed all of our lives. The main change in my life, as I was locked down with the rest of the United Kingdom, was having too much time and too little to do. Out of tragedy, sometimes light shines on other aspects of life. This is what happened to me during covid. Encouraged strongly by my friend, CV, to write a full autobiography of my life's adventures, I eventually decided instead to write a few short stories, stories which are remembrances of some of the international adventures I experienced over many years. I started writing my first story in April 2020.

The most important decision of my life was to apply to join the U.S. Peace Corps, which had been established by President Kennedy in March 1961. After completing my legal education at the Harvard Law School in June 1966, I was accepted by the Peace Corps and sent to Syracuse University in September 1966 to train as a secondary school teacher in the program designated as Malawi X. My fellow trainees and I arrived in Malawi on January 1, 1967.

I have now lived 39 of the past 58 years of my life in Malawi, Kenya, Russia and the United Kingdom. My work and other international travel has taken me to 99 countries during these years. All because I applied to be a Peace Corps Volunteer in 1966. None of this was planned or anticipated; it just happened. I have been blessed and would not change any of my past.

London, United Kingdom
October 2024
Email: smatterings42@gmail.com

CONTENTS

CHOLO ADVENTURE

Kwacha. Dawn. Birdsong. The African symphony. Before the first streaks of morning sunshine, the avian chorus heralds the day. Like being brought out of a deep sleep by a soft, warmly moving, musical massage. Life is good; slowly and drowsily you become aware of your existence each African morn.

Today was to be unique. May 7th, in our youth, more than a half century ago. It was early. Dave and I slept the previous night at a forestry station in Cholo, Malawi. We agreed with Jones, a Welsh forestry and game officer working for the Malawi Government, to spend a week helping to build a road in the middle of – well, nowhere. Jones drove us there on Sunday afternoon from Blantyre in a short wheelbase, government Land Rover. This was our first school break project. All Peace Corps teachers were asked to undertake special projects during school holidays.

Sweet tea and bananas. Breakfast. In t-shirts, the ubiquitous shorts and sneakers, we were ready at 6 a.m. Monday to begin the three mile trek, downhill, to the construction site. We had to be there at 7 a.m. We trod down the dusty, reddish dirt road, avoiding rocks and ruts in the road. The rainy season had ended so the uneven surface of the road was without pools of water and mosquitoes. Around us stretched the lush African bush painted with varied shades of green, some deep, some dark and others soft and almost washed of green.

Only the plants near the road were red-dusted from the few vehicles that frequented this lonely road.

The soft sunlight of the early morn, in the middle of central Africa, was far from anywhere. Dave and I thought we were alone. Or were we? We only saw the bush; but more than the bush saw us. Unseen, small villages were waking up, humming with village murmurings, and brimming with the light of wafting, white smoke from the recently lit breakfast fires. We appeared to be alone, but in reality, we were now players on the stage of an African morning.

It would be hard for two mzungus (white men) to disappear in the middle of Africa. Our noisy plodding and yakking were heard as we walked downhill. Every so often, white-toothed smiles of small children emerged unexpectedly from the bush -- on the side of the road. Our progress was noticed, monitored and commented on. We said moni, the Malawian hello, to each little group of children whom we met from time to time. All were barefoot, and their shirts and dresses were patched or torn. Their screams, smiles and dances were reminiscent of children reacting to unexpected visitors anywhere in rural Malawi. I wondered if David Livingstone was similarly greeted as his footprint was left in Africa in general and Malawi in particular.

It took about an hour each day to reach the construction site which was located about a hundred meters off to the right of the road. There we met about a dozen road workers, including Bwanali, the kapitao (foreman). All greeted us with the Malawian moni welcome, with their digging implements in hand. Dave and I spoke a bit of Chinyanja; the forest workers spoke only Chinyanja. Smiles and head nodding go only so far in uniting peoples who speak different languages.

Bwanali issued each of us with a short-handled hoe. These were to become our friends and enemies over the next week. To use such a hoe, we had to bend our knees and lower our backs, as we swung the hoe into the ground and pulled the earth back from the side of the hill. The hill sloped downward at a steep angle so the idea was to start stripping the dirt away at a place where the road would eventually appear. Bwanali made the decision where to dig. He knew where and how wide the road had to be. Then he stood to the side and the road gang took over. We worked in small groups to unzip the hill of its dirt cover and over time eat into the hill so that a road would appear. The higher up the hill we dug, the more difficult it was to maintain our balance and to remove the dirt without covering another worker below with dirt from the pull of each stroke of the hoe.

This required coordination. This required planning. And this required our soft, teacher's bodies to compete with seasoned road workers, whose hands were calloused, whose arms and legs were wiry and muscled for this type of work and whose skills with a short-handled hoe far exceeded what Dave and I would ever be able to achieve. We were at the bottom of the building ladder, in skill, in strength and in the ability to repeat the same motion over and over and over for hours at a time throughout the day and week.

All this took place from 7 a.m. each morning until about 1 p.m. in the afternoon; under the relentless glare of the African sun, which made the end of our work day many degrees hotter than when we began.

We had few short breaks during each six hour work day when we shared water, bananas and sugar cane with our road gang colleagues. And best of all, we had a chance to sit in the shade and rest our weary arms and legs. During breaks our colleagues yammered with each other in an endless stream of Chinyanja. We tried to interact, but the language barrier prevented us from being able to communicate meaningfully with each other.

While we worked, our colleagues would sing songs which we didn't know or understand. And their endless banter was no doubt frequently directed at us – two mzungus, working on a road gang in the middle of the hot, African bush. Imagine their thoughts. What had the mzungus done wrong? Were they prisoners let out for a week of work? Were they being punished for something that the workers couldn't understand? Dave and I were the Mutt and Jeff of the road gang; two clumsy, unskilled mzungus forced to build a forestry road. There had to be a back story --but not one which would be understood by our gregarious road gang colleagues.

The road we helped construct was not only in the middle of nowhere, it appeared to be going – nowhere. The bush was wild, extensive and never-ending. The steep hill itself was part of the East African Rift Valley, which meanders from the Red Sea through Ethiopia, Kenya and Tanzania to reach Malawi and Cholo. The road would curve around the hill, like a belt on the waist of this giant dirt being. There was no obvious place the road would end. We started working at the beginning and wouldn't be with the road gang long enough to see the results of our labours. Whether the road was part of a plan to transport people, bananas, timber or other commodities, we would never know. It was just our road, our project, our mission, our commitment, our pain.

Walking to the construction site was a pleasure each morning. The cool morning breeze, the chorus of birds and youngsters, and the downhill direction of travel made a refreshing start to the day.

Returning to the forest station each afternoon after six hours of endless, sweaty, back-breaking and leg-tiring work was much less so. Each day, when the sun was near its zenith, Bwanali told us all to stop. Dave and I said tsalani bwino (stay well) to each of our road gang colleagues and began the most excruciating part of our day; trudging uphill for three miles at the hottest time of the day, after we had used up all our energy to play our small part in the reconfiguration of a lonely hill in a remote part of Africa.

One day, on our slow meander up the road, we spotted a grove of extremely tall banana trees off to the side. This was not a commercial plantation, rather a bunch of sky-reaching trees which must have been planted by villagers many years before, given their heights. Even more remarkable than the tall banana trees, which was evident to us after only five months in the country, was the length of the individual banana leaves. These were spectacularly different from their smaller cousins all over the rest of Malawi. We walked off the road and went over to the grove. I picked up a heavy leaf which was at least twice my height. The rubbery banana leaf, still green with its usual capricious edges, stood straight and tall in my hands, casting a shadow over me, but not over the thrill of my discovery. The photo that Dave snapped of me on that hot May afternoon has remained locked in my memory.

On that first day, May 7th, the trek home was particularly painful. It was the first day we had worked on the road. We had not prepared ourselves for the physical effort that six hours of short-handle hoeing would require. Each step back to the forest station was more difficult than the previous one. Step by step by step. Exhaustion. Pain. Sweat. Heat. Uphill. Relentless. Repeat.

What greeted us at the end of this uphill trudge was the shade of the forestry station and the friendliness of its two occupants who made our stay more than bearable. In charge was João, a giant of a man from Mozambique. I met over the years only one other man with fingers of his size, the Prime Minister of Lesotho, Chief Leabua Jonathan. But that was to be three years hence. When João shook your hand, it was lost, gone, unseen, as within a soft pillow. He may have been a large man, but the softness and serenity of his personality which endeared him to us was reflected in the comfort of his pleasurable handshake.

João spoke Portuguese and was relatively fluent in Chinyanja; more relatively fluent in Chinyanja than we were. Even though we had minimal local language capability, we spent the late afternoons and evenings together, talking with mouth and hands about all manner of things, mundane and beyond, as people do who are thrown together in the boat of life. João was full of stories, about himself, his life, Mozambique, Malawi and his view of the world. His round face lit up when he smiled, and he laughed with amusement, abandon and enjoyment. He was at peace with his place in life.

Assisting João was a teenage Malawian boy, Kamwendo, who undertook whatever chores João asked of him, Like most teenage boys who are faced with mzungus for the first time in their lives, Kamwendo was shy and reluctant to speak. He hung about in the shadows, no doubt marvelling at the ability of João and the two mzungus to do daily damage to his lingua franca.

Notwithstanding his management responsibilities, João was also the chief cook and bottle washer at the forestry station. While he cooked nsima (corn meal) and ndiwo (vegetables or meat) each evening, we sat around the fire with him, talking of cabbages and kings, or at least attempting to do so. We asked about his life; he reciprocated and wanted to know about us, where we came from and why we were there. We tried to explain to him the back story, the reason two mzungus were spending time in the centre of the African bush. I'm not sure our Chinyanja capabilities ever brought understanding to his reasonable enquiries.

These languid late afternoons and evenings were the perfect antidote to the relentless and endless pace of our weary workdays. The fire was not just a focal point for our nightly rendezvous and food requirements. It was chilly in the evening at that time of year and the jumping flames were a soporific for our intense efforts of the day.

The pattern for our week's stay at the forest station was set that first day. Every day we woke up, dressed and ate, and happily made the downhill voyage. However, we struggled to survive the three mile walk back. The first place we landed upon arrival back at the forest station was where we slept. We collapsed upon our beds, unable to speak. Closed our eyes and went into our respective dreamlands. After a short (or not so short) nap, we each showered, even welcoming the warm, almost hot water over our tired and dirty bodies, though we would have preferred a colder alternative. We washed the dirt, the heat, the sweat, the remnants of the hill off of ourselves. And then we sat with João to eat and share our nightly ritual.

The ablution facilities at the forest camp were divided into a showering place with a wash basin and a separate, grass hut with a pointed roof for our daily and necessary functions. The simple, khaki-coloured grass hut had a cement floor; in the middle was a nine inch round hole. Similar facilities were common all over Africa and Malawi, but not in the teacher's homes in which we had been comfortably settled. So, approaching the round hole required dexterity, the ability to centre oneself and the willingness and strength to withstand the ever-present reminder of previous visits to the round-holed hut. Ridding oneself of water and beer detritus was less challenging. Squatting over the round hole, while maintaining balance and direction, may have been a simple feat for millions of others, but to us it required a gymnast's abilities to successfully achieve the goal.

In my case, with difficulty and not less than constant complaints about the facilities, I was able to add my daily contribution through the round hole. The process was unfamiliar and led to some awkward moments; but I had a high success rate. Dave, on the other hand, found the round hole and the squatting requirement to be intimidating and beyond his capabilities. Not to elaborate the point, Dave over the seven days of our work week was unable to use the round hole as intended. Not once. As if some part of his body said nope, not here, no way; I'll take the punishment of waiting. And wait he did. Only upon our return to Blantyre at the end of the week was Dave able to find solace on a traditional toilet seat in my teacher's house on which he read a not too recent Time Magazine during his one hour visit to the facilities. No wonder many call it a comfort station. It surely was for Dave.

Our last day of work on the road was an emotional one. During the week, Dave and I had strengthened every part of our bodies, especially our arms and legs. We had lost weight, burned all uncovered skin parts, and no doubt more through osmosis than education, spoke more Chinyanja than we did before. We were on the road gang; a strange appendage to their little unit, but in our minds, we had become essential parts of this road building crew. I remember taking pride in certain sections of the road on which I worked; these were "my" parts of the road and I proudly showed them to Dave and others, evidence of a contribution that a week earlier I would never have imagined. Our last tsalani bwinos lingered in the air as we departed for the forestry station the last afternoon. Decades later, I feel that nostalgia as I write these words.

This small project was the essence of the Peace Corps. I didn't know it at the time but participating in the Cholo experience was indicative of why I joined this amazing team of committed Americans, donating a part of their early lives to the most unfamiliar parts of the world.

It would be easier to describe this feeling to those who were privileged to have lived during the life and presidency of John F. Kennedy, and who watched the birth and growth of the Peace Corps, one of the core aspects of the Kennedy international relations program. It would be almost impossible to do so to those who came later and who encountered neither Kennedy, nor the Peace Corps nor its raison d'etre. To have lived the Peace Corps ideal does not mean one could easily communicate it to others, to those who had not undertaken the same venture into the unknown. Some things in life can only be told through shared and common experiences. Every RPCV (returned Peace Corps Volunteer) knows this.

The drive back to Blantyre with Jones on that Sunday afternoon forever cut our connection with the soon-to-be new road in Cholo, but not with the memories of our adventure which have lasted over so many years. The ninety minute drive brought us from our quiet forestry refuge to the hustle and bustle of Blantyre, Malawi's largest city, the vibrant commercial centre of the country. It was in fact as vast and far-ranging a journey as the one we had initially made from America to Malawi itself.

Completed: May 30, 2020

QUEST FOR QUELIMANE

An Easter Story 1967

Events just happen. Not every decision has a road map. Or a GPS connection. Especially in the Peace Corps. Unsurprisingly, Peace Corps Volunteers worldwide know this. One day you are teaching English in a classroom in Blantyre, Malawi. The next day you are visiting Quelimane, Mozambique. As one does. No plan. We just went. We hired a Land Rover; we drove to Quelimane. We drove back to Blantyre. It happened.

It was our first break in the 1967 school calendar, a four-day Easter weekend holiday. No teaching required. No grading of papers. No late night preparation of lesson plans. No red-eyed early mornings. No muddy path or road to walk on to get to the classroom. No sleepy heads on desks in the afternoon. Four days of rest on the horizon.

The holiday came at an emotional time for us. It was near the end of our first term of teaching secondary school. We had spent the past two months adjusting to our new roles as secondary school teachers and, even more so, to living in an African country for the first time in our lives. All of us were away from our families and our culture, a separation which we overcame through our enthusiasm for the job we had applied for and were trained to do. This took energy, which needed reinvigoration from the upcoming holiday.

On March 19, a few days before the Easter holiday, the Peace Corps Director in Malawi, Will, his wife Jane and their four boys, left Malawi at the end of Will's two-year contract. In the upstairs, gone-to-seed departure lounge of Chileka Airport, over two hundred hardy souls, sweating and drinking together in the hot, cramped space of the lounge, met to wish the Lotter family a safe journey and a successful future in their home State of California. The assemblage included the US Ambassador, Marshall P Jones and his ubiquitous baseball cap, the head of the US Information Service, the US Army representative and numerous Peace Corps Volunteers who happened in be in Blantyre on that auspicious day.

Will was the only Director we had known. He had visited Syracuse in our first week of training the previous September, to start the process of making us into Peace Corps Volunteers in Malawi. He next met us on January 1st at the bottom of the stairs as we de-planed in Blantyre from an East African Airways Comet. He and his team had helped integrate our Malawi X group into the fabric of the Peace Corps in Malawi. Will and Jane hosted pancake breakfasts at their home every Sunday from the date of their arrival in Malawi until the date of their departure. Who would have ever thought that pancakes would be part of the glue which brought us all together as a Peace Corps family? One of our beacons as we sailed the seas of a new life in Malawi was about to disappear.

Preparation for the Trip

The plan to visit Quelimane originated, like Topsy, from the minds of the four Peace Corps Volunteers teaching at Henry Henderson Institute (HHI), the largest day secondary school in Blantyre. Three were members of Malawi VIII, and had been teaching at HHI for a year. I was the only member of Malawi X, the newest and most inexperienced of this teacher corps. There was John, my roommate, a teacher of history; Sandy, a teacher of English; Arlee, a teacher of science and math; and myself, a neophyte teaching English for students about to take the dreaded Cambridge leaving exam.

Henry Henderson Institute (HHI) is an educational establishment, originally founded in 1909. It was named in honour of Henry Henderson (1843-91), a lay missionary of the Church of Scotland, who founded the Blantyre Mission. The original establishment included a primary school, a teacher training college, a theological college, and a technical college to teach practical skills such as carpentry, bricklaying and printing. It also served as printer for the Blantyre Mission, producing religious texts, school textbooks, and government and other daily and weekly publications. In the late 1950s, the secondary school was opened at the site.

HHI lies within the grounds of St Michael and All Angels Church, which was_constructed of red brick from 1888 to 1891 at the Blantyre Mission. The church was designed, and its construction managed, by Rev. David Clement Scott, who had no formal architectural training. Labour was provided by local men who had no previous experience in this type of construction. All the bricks used in the church were made on-site from local clay and fired in wood-fueled kilns.

To carry out our intention to get away from HHI and to Quelimane over Easter, we needed a car. More specifically we needed a Land Rover as we were told that the roads in Mozambique were badly maintained, requiring off road manoeuvring capability. A simple solution presented itself. One of our fellow teachers at HHI had a Land Rover. A bit of sweet talking from Sandy and Arlee helped us to arrange a rental of the Land Rover over the Easter weekend.

In truth, we had to prevaricate a bit to ensure we could rent this Land Rover for the trip. There had been intense rains in Mozambique that year, where floods were reported in many parts of that country. Our benefactor (owner of the Land Rover) insisted that we stay in Malawi as he knew about the floods in Mozambique; he also knew that many people went there for the Easter holidays. We told him that we planned to go to Salima, a holiday site on the shores of Lake Malawi, for our Easter trip. Upon our return, we told him that we went to Salima and had a great time at the Lake. He said that we made the right choice as much of Mozambique was flooded from the heavy rains.

As a short-wheel base Land Rover can hold seven passengers and their katundu (baggage), we needed to find three more people to participate in our Easter adventure. We recruited two in the form of Steve and Mary, a lovely couple who were teaching at Dedza Day Secondary School. Our last passenger was Emil, a Welsh forester serving in the Malawi Government who had befriended several of us Volunteers. Emil had arrived in Malawi two months before our arrival, and was already in sync with the country and its people.

Our intrepid gang of seven filled every nook and cranny of the Land Rover, counting bodies and baggage. We brought a bit of water and food with us, and sleeping bags as we had no idea where we would spend the nights; perhaps at the beach itself. Such are the dreams of Peace Corps Volunteers.

The Trip Begins

At 6:15 am on Good Friday morning, March 24, we left HHI and headed toward Mlanje, a town in the lower southeast of Malawi which has a border post with Mozambique. The one-hour drive on a firm, smooth, well packed dirt road was uneventful. Once at the border post in Mlanje, we had to go through immigration and customs. In a few minutes, we were in Milange, the Mozambique town twinned with Mlanje. Milange is the District Centre of Zambezia Province, located on the western side of Mozambique, in the middle of the country. Because we were only half awake, we stopped for a coffee and a bite to eat to get us ready for the remaining three hundred thirty kilometer (200 mile) day trip to Quelimane.

Why Quelimane? One of its attractions was the history of this near coastal city. Vasco da Gama, on his way to India in 1498, named the river that goes from the coast to the city the "River of the Good Signs", as he saw "good signs" at that point in his voyage that he was on the right path to India. For us, a trip away from Malawi to the Indian Ocean coast was also a good sign. Centuries later Quelimane was the end point of one of the greatest feats of exploration of the 19th century, David Livingstone's west-to-east crossing of south-central Africa in 1856. It was now to be the end point of our Easter holiday, and break from our teaching roles in Malawi.

The dirt road in Mozambique was much rougher than the road which we had travelled on in Malawi. Potholes everywhere, rocks in the road, ruts from the rains; it was hard to build up any speed. The first sixty kilometres were an unbelievably difficult drive. We were proud that the dirt roads in Malawi were better maintained, easier to navigate. However, soon after, the road surfaces improved and it was smooth sailing for the next part of the trip.

Mozambique had been known before as P.E.A., Portuguese East Africa. The development of the country by the Portuguese was quite different from the British approach in Malawi. Almost all of the country consisted of bush, undeveloped and without urban or semi-urban areas. Not even small towns. We would often drive thirty minutes before we saw a person walking on the road. This would have been impossible in Malawi, where people were always seen on any road.

All of this changed when one reached the coastal areas of the country. Adjacent to the Indian Ocean, the great cities of Mozambique are located: Lorenzo Marques, Beira and Quelimane. These cities were imitations of their counterparts in Portugal, with four-laned boulevards as the main street, separated by old, tall palm trees indicating that they had been there for decades. Multi-story buildings were everywhere, a stark contrast to the few one could find in the main cities of Malawi.

As we drove through the country, we saw that the land was poorer than land in Malawi, the crops were poorer than crops in Malawi, the clothing worn by the few people we saw was poorer than the clothing we saw people wearing in Malawi. No one in the bush had shoes. Most women were bare breasted. Men wore something like a bark jockstrap as their form of dress. It felt like we had driven back in time to a less modern and connected society. The Malawi bush contained more activity and people than the Mozambique bush.

Portuguese Army Post

After driving sixty kilometres from Milange, which took us almost two hours on the pock-marked road, we noticed we were low on petrol. We hadn't filled up in

Milange for some reason, perhaps the inattention of young Volunteers more focused on what they were seeing than on ensuring that their trip was safe. Fortuitously we drove by a Portuguese army post at this exact point. The consensus quickly reached amongst us was to stop and ask to buy petrol from the soldiers.

At that time, there were about one hundred thousand Portuguese soldiers in Angola and Mozambique. The fabric of the Portuguese empire in Africa was unravelling, disintegrating, collapsing, and the only way to hold on to the vestiges of colonialism was to use hard power in the form of guns, bullets and boots.

The festering opposition to Portuguese colonialism was in the form of anti-government movements. The main opposition movement in Mozambique was called FRELIMO, the Mozambique Liberation Front. It was founded by Eduardo Mondlane, a Harvard Ph.D. who had been an assistant professor at Syracuse University, married to an American. He left the comfort of life at Syracuse University after being elected President of FRELIMO in 1962. The next year he moved to Tanzania where FRELIMO had set up training facilities for the eventual guerrilla war conducted by Mondlane and his FRELIMO associates. His life was considerably shortened on February 3, 1969, when he opened a book in a package while at his FRELIMO training headquarters in Tanzania. The book was a bomb which exploded, killing him outright. No charges were ever brought against the perpetrators.

The soldiers we met at the army post were welcoming, no doubt because we broke the monotony of their existence in the middle of the Mozambique bush. To celebrate our arrival, they broke out a bottle of 1920 Portuguese brandy to share with us. It was fortunate that we were all drinking brandy as communication between us was difficult. Thankfully Emil spoke some Spanish and a soldier named Manuel was able to speak some Chinyanja; just like us. Using our hands and smiles, these were the only ways we could speak with our new friends. Lots of laughs and smiles and jokes filled the time we were there. A soldier even climbed an orange tree at the army post to harvest oranges to be shared with us.

We spent two hours in the comfort of the army post, perhaps influenced by the soporific effect of the well-aged brandy. Manuel and his colleagues wanted us to stay longer, but the quest of reaching the coastal town of Quelimane by the end of the day was our inspiration to leave. We promised to stop and chat with them on our way back to Malawi a couple days later. After many hugs and with much reluctance, we returned to the Land Rover and its uncomfortable springs.

Town of Mocuba

Our friends at the army post told us we had to drive through another one hundred thirty kilometres of endless bush to reach the town of Mocuba. As our Land Rover bounced along the dirt road, we chatted and sang and enjoyed the view of the green, Mozambique bush. Time went by quickly, and soon we spotted a town, a real town. What we didn't expect was how wonderful Mocuba would prove to be.

Even in the 1960s, Mocuba was a large town in the middle of the route from Malawi to Quelimane. It had a well-developed market area, and an impressive three hundred metre-long bridge over the wide, gently flowing Licungo River. We were in the middle of the Mozambique bush, but had found a town with paved streets, a central boulevard, tall palm trees separating the lanes in town and lights on elegantly Portuguese-designed posts. We took our time (maybe the brandy was still at work), and had a two-hour lunch break. We drank 2M Beer, ate piri-piri prawns. Sitting in the shade on a hot afternoon, we were living the life. Mocuba was the perfect break in our journey. However, Quelimane beckoned. At 2:30 pm, with a filled gas tank and happily filled tummies, we were back in the Land Rover and driving again through the relentless bush. We finally arrived in Quelimane at 6 pm that evening, speeded by the fifty kilometres of paved road as we neared the city.

Quelimane: Our Destination

As we pulled into the city, certainly not a town, our spirits improved. But first, a practical problem. We had no place to spend the night. Our gas tank was low, so we drove into a gas station to fill up the tank. We asked the person pumping our gas where we might find a hotel for the night. Because it was Easter weekend, we were told that it would be unlikely to find hotel rooms that night. The gas station man said he knew one hotel that might have rooms: the Hotel Quelimane. Although not very original in name, it was to become our haven and comfort for the next couple days.

Luck was with us. The hotel had its last two rooms available, at a cost of £1.10 ($3.10) per night each. This price included three meals a day, dinner being a six-course bonanza, the first night highlighted by steak and wine. We did have one small problem; how to distribute the seven of us into the two rooms. Steve and Mary made it easy for us by agreeing be apart at night. We had one room for men, one room for women, as proposed by Emil. Three ladies in one room; four men in the other. It worked. We were exhausted after our twelve-hour journey. After a hearty and tasty meal, we headed to our rooms and disappeared into our respective dreamlands.

The next morning was a Saturday. Since the stores were going to close on Sunday and Monday, we went shopping that morning. I splurged and bought a pair of hiking boots. Why? It was my birthday, one of many I have spent over the years on the African continent. John and I also bought a gallon of Portuguese wine for Sh13/3 ($1.35) in escudos. This was a present to both of us, which we lugged back to Blantyre when we returned.

Walking through the city, we noted that the architecture was very European, with a distinctive Portuguese flavour. The buildings echoed the pastel colours that one sees in every Portuguese city and town. When we reached the picturesque harbour, we walked along a promenade near the water. Quelimane is located on the Cuacua River, not far from the Indian Ocean. The smell of the ocean was ever present in the air, as we enjoyed our morning stroll together in a new city.

It's a Lota Beach

Upon returning to the hotel, we picked up the box lunches we had ordered that morning, the cost of which was included in the price of our room at the hotel. We were now ready to hit the beach northeast of the city. The beach is called Praia de Zalata (Zalata Beach). The road to Zalata Beach was even worse than the one we first encountered upon leaving Milange. So bad was the road that it took us forty-five minutes to drive the eighteen miles to reach the coast. But there were other wonders to see on this short trip.

To get to Zalata Beach, we had to drive through what might have been the largest coconut plantations in the world, certainly larger than any of us had ever seen. There seemed like a billion trees, planted row upon row upon row upon row, with many, small roads amidst the trees to facilitate the harvesting of the coconuts. We also saw several villages in the midst of the plantations. These villages reminded us of Malawi, although with rice paddies instead of maize fields. The people in the villages seemed stoic and quiet as we drove through, without the energy and openness which we had witnessed in our short time in Malawi.

The coconut trees we encountered on our drive to the beach were planted into seven enormous blocks to ease the annual harvesting. The land around Quelimane was flat and green, with lots of water in small ponds and streams. This was in contrast to the land around Milange which was full of high hills, culminating in the spectre of Mount Mlanje, a ten-thousand-foot giant in the middle of the rolling, hilly countryside. During the long road trip from Milange to Quelimane, the land was hilly, only flattening as we neared the coast.

We were amazed by the beach when we got there. We parked on a spot near the changing huts made of grass and located above beach level. We sat there, open mouthed. There were more than one hundred yards of open beach before one reached the water. The sand was bright white, making it difficult to see in the middle of the day without sunglasses. Looking north and south, the beach went on for miles and miles in each direction, yet all we could see were six other people on the beach when we got there. It was pristine, nature untouched by man. It was Miami Beach, without hotels. Which no doubt would come.

We were starving, so as soon as we changed into our bathing suits, we ate our box lunches. Some 2M Beer and Peace Corps banter helped the food to flow to our tummies. Then it was off to the sand, and the water.

There were crabs all over the beach. They didn't like the attention we gave them. The water was warm, and walking into the water was like walking a gentle slope, slowly rising to our knees. We then swam in the Indian Ocean, played games on the beach, enjoying this fantastic setting as if we were the only people in the world. Each of us was enthralled by the beauty of the beach and the fact that there were almost no people on the planet to enjoy it.

But, all good things come to an end. By mid-afternoon, the tide started to come in. Within about an hour, we couldn't even see the beach. It was totally covered by the ocean. We climbed up a little hill just above the beach and watched the tide as it rolled in. With the warm water and beautiful weather, we found the perfect spot for rejuvenation. This was exactly the reason we had come to Quelimane. And, for me, it was my birthday, a most unusual birthday gift.

The drive back through the plantation was more relaxed. We had reached our objective, a beach holiday at Easter. The 2M Beer was also doing its job, helping us to relax. We had a meal at the hotel, and everyone except John and me went up to sleep. We made other plans, as part of my birthday bash. We asked the hotel concierge where we might get some drinks that night and he recommended the White Cock Bar, an appropriately named enterprise. Along with five other people at the hotel, we meandered over to the Bar. It was a surprise finding people of all shades enjoying the evening together: whites, Africans and assimilados, a coloured mix which was so named by the Mozambique Government to allow non-whites to share the benefits of being "Portuguese" without having political rights. A sop to the rest of the international community which frowned on such appellations and pretences.

On Saturday's Easter eve, Arlee, Mary and Steve, the more religious of our little group, attended midnight mass at a local Catholic church. The celebrants considerably outnumbered the available places and space inside. Our holiday venturers had to stand on the steps of the church during the service, which ended early Sunday morning.

We all had a long sleep on Easter Sunday morning, especially Arlee, Mary and Steve who had attended late mass the night before. We awoke and shared another filling and tasty breakfast. After breakfast and a walk about the town, we got ready for our second day at Zalata Beach. Another forty-five minute ride through the coconut plantations continued to amaze us as we scanned the endless, really endless, rows and rows of coconut trees.

The weather was again warm and sunny. We swam in the ocean, played football, sat under the shade of some trees near the place we parked the car and talked about our lives and experiences since we had joined the Peace Corps. It was a day of relaxation and enjoyment, again all alone on one of the most beautiful beaches in the world. Our ride back to the hotel was sad as we realized that this was the end of the fun part of the trip. All that remained before us was the long drive back to Malawi and our teaching posts.

Sunday night we drank 2M Beer at the Hotel Quelimane bar. As was the habit in Quelimane at that time, the purchase of a beer entitled one to eat clams, sardines, lobster, spicy prawns, and fried pieces of coconut, all without payment. These were the sides for the bottles of 2M Beer we bought. Were we in heaven? The Portuguese business sense was not as venal as the British; beer was meant to have sides that one didn't have to pay for.

After our drinking and side dishes, we stayed on the porch of the hotel and had a coffee. To top it off, a bit of brandy to put into the coffee. It wasn't 1920 brandy, but good nevertheless. If we had been smokers, it would have been time to light up a cigar. Somehow, we survived without such an extravagance.

Back to Malawi

The next morning, now Easter Monday, we got up early to have breakfast, which included a full table of food with coffee and tea. After filling up the gas tank, we left Quelimane at 8:30 am. To ensure that we would make the trip without any risk, we bought two four-gallon cans of gas to take with us. The smell in the car wasn't the same as at the beach, but at least it wouldn't be a lack of fuel that would prevent us from returning to Malawi.

The weather changed that Monday morning. It started to rain and continued to rain through much of the trip back home. Because of the rain and the condition of the roads, we often travelled at a speeds of fifteen-twenty miles per hour. Another reason for our slow progress is that the Land Rover's windscreen wipers didn't work. The person sitting next to the driver had to reach out through the side window and move the wipers by hand. Not the most efficient way to keep the windscreen clear. Also, with the bad weather our luck changed. A flat tire greeted us along the way. When changing the tire, it took less than a minute for the car to be surrounded by dozens of villagers who came out of nowhere in the bush to stand and watch us replace the tire.

We went through Mocuba again, and stopped for more 2M Beer and food. This time, since it was raining, we decided to move on soon after eating. We passed the soldier's post again; the same one we saw on the way down. We stopped to chat with Manuel and his friends and to give them cigarettes to thank them for their hospitality when we first met them. We were going to take photos of the soldiers and ourselves but decided not to. They were in the middle of a war zone and we weren't sure how the soldiers would react to our taking photographs. The photographs that are available to me today are my memories, in my mind, as I recall with much affection and happiness the time we spent with these otherwise forlorn soldiers.

The rest of the drive was almost routine, slow but routine. When we finally got to Milange, we sped through customs and immigration. But on the Malawi side, we decided to stop for one more 2M Beer. We were back home and would miss the taste of our Portuguese nectar. After our beers, it was an hour ride back to Blantyre and home.

We washed the Land Rover at our house before returning it the next morning to the owner of the car. The story of our visit to Salima on Lake Malawi was told with smiles and sniggers, unnoticed by our benefactor. We told him of all that we did at the Lake, and what we saw and ate. We also confirmed that we had not left the country (we had removed the gallon jugs of Portuguese wine from the car before returning it). He said that he was happy that we had avoided the rains of Mozambique.

The four-day trip, including the cost of renting the car, purchasing gas, food and two hotel rooms for two nights, had cost us £13/6 ($37.40) -- for all of us. Just over $5 each. A real Peace Corps triumph.

It is now fifty-four years later. In visiting ninety-nine countries, I have experienced many unusual parts of the world in my life. I have seen more than most and met some of the most interesting characters one could imagine on these travels. But the Quelimane quest sits high on my list of remembered adventures. Maybe it was because it was the first visit outside Malawi, the first time I had to use my passport again. Maybe it was because it was also my birthday weekend. And maybe it was because I was with my Peace Corps mates and friends, with whom I shared the intense Peace Corps experience that all Volunteers are fortunate to share. But mostly, beyond the 2M Beer, the 1920 brandy, the coconut plantations, the endless uninhabited, white beach, the friendships of my colleagues and the ambiance of a Portuguese city, I remember returning to Blantyre, my home. I learned quickly that home is where you live, not where you are from. And Malawi was exactly that, the place I hung my hat --and with John, finished the gallon of Portuguese wine that we brought back home.

Completed: January 10, 2021

KILIMANJARO CLIMB

Kilimanjaro. A name which evokes a massive presence, a challenge, a heavenly power, a home of the gods. Capped by a snow-white boa in the middle of Africa. A disputed name, which changes meaning depending upon whether one is Chagga, or Kamba, or Masai or Swahili. And even then, the meaning of the name is lost in the mists of time and in the minds of the 19th century male, European explorers who often misunderstood what they heard from their African sources. Kilimanjaro.

Since the days of the 19th century when the East African region was visited by the intrepid explorers, more of the geology of Mt. Kilimanjaro has been studied and is known. Mt. Kilimanjaro is a dormant stratovolcano in Tanzania, composed of three distinct volcanic cones: Kibo, the highest at 19,341 feet; Mawenzi at 16,893 feet; and Shira at 13,140 feet. It is the highest mountain in Africa and the highest single free-standing mountain in the world, proudly reaching many thousands of feet above its plateau base. Mawenzi and Shira are extinct, while Kibo is dormant and could erupt again.

Kilimanjaro is distinct from the mountains of Malawi, the largest of which is known as the Mulanje Massif (it was called Mlanje in 1967, but as happens in many African countries, names change as politicians come and go). The Mulanje Massif was formed by the intrusion of magma into the earth's crust about one hundred thirty million years ago. The surrounding rock eroded away over time, leaving behind the erosion-resistant igneous rock of the Mulanje Massif itself. It stands proudly above the plain below. It rises dramatically above the landscape near Lake Chilwa, a shallow, saline lake below Lake Malawi. The upper slopes of the Mulanje Massif are a protected forest. The deep green colour south of the Mulanje Massif results from the tea and macadamia farms scattered along the mountain's flanks.

Almost all mountains of Malawi are like the Mulanje Massif, erosion-resistant igneous rocks with sharp and deep cliffs and chasms that dot the Malawi landscape. There is nothing like Mt. Kilimanjaro in Malawi. The highest point of the Mulanje Massif is Sapitwa, 3,000 metres (9,850 feet) above the plain. It is impossible to see Sapitwa from the ground as it is mostly often lost in the mists, clouds and rain which frequent the higher levels of the mountain without rhyme or reason.

David Livingstone first mentioned the Mulanje Massif in his writings in 1859, but there is little doubt that Stone Age peoples, known as the Akufula, were living around the Mulanje Massif in the mists of the history of the region. As far as mountains in Africa are concerned, this is all we knew before we ventured north to Tanzania and our Kilimanjaro adventure.

It was the middle of December 1967, at the end of my first year as a Peace Corps Volunteer teaching in Malawi. A group of us had decided earlier in the year to climb Mt. Kilimanjaro in Tanzania during the December school holidays. We had all finished the last term of the school year in early December and did not have to be back to teach again until mid-January 1968. All assignments had been finished, all grading completed; it was time for us teachers to get away from our classes and do something unique. For my friends and me, it was time to venture out into Africa.

Who amongst us suggested that we should climb Mt. Kilimanjaro during our school holidays? Probably the main instigator was Dave, who had climbed three substantial mountains in the US in the previous three years. During Peace Corps training he made us aware that the opportunity to climb Mt. Kilimanjaro existed. While we treated this as light-hearted banter during training in Syracuse in the Fall of 1966, at some point in 1967, it became a real obsession. As to making the travel and climbing arrangements, there was no internet to find out information about how one would arrange the details of the trip. We had no phones. We had little money. And yet, all of us were able to find our ways from our various teaching posts scattered about Malawi to the pinnacle of Africa. This is not a unique story, but from the point of view of the world over fifty years later, it is an interesting one.

On the morning of December 15th, we gathered at Chileka Airport in Blantyre (the only international airport in Malawi at that time). The one air carrier flying to Dar-es-Salaam (Dar) was East African Airways, and the specific aircraft we boarded was the same de

Havilland Comet in which we had flown from Dar to Blantyre on January 1, 1967, the date we first landed in Malawi. Anxious and excited travellers all, it was our first international flight since we arrived in the country.

We had been committed to the localities and people of our respective homes, almost all in rural Malawi. We had done what the Peace Corps asked of us; we became part of the fabric of the small societies in which each of us lived. We brought an American insight into life onto the rural African stage. To do this, we had to cut ties with our past, our families, our former lives and loves, and in return, jump into the middle and muddle of our new local lives. In our different ways, we all experienced a fascinating year, many trials and tribulations, many new friendships and participation in the day-to-day of our local school communities. This required effort, concentration and long days and nights, often under the soft, yellow glare of an Aladdin (paraffin) lamp. It was now time to break away from our new homes for a few weeks, and to expand our African horizons.

The flight was uneventful, yet for those of us who had been home bound for almost a year, it was exhilarating. As we soared over Lake Malawi on a partly cloudy morning, our love for the country we had served for a year was combined with the expectations of the holiday ahead of us. From the plane we could see the familiar shape of the blue beauty for which the country was named. The sun reflected on the lake's waters, showering our eyes with many gleaming jewels interspersed among the soft, white clouds through which we meandered. We were leaving a lifestyle which had become familiar and entering the beginning of an adventure previously experienced by the likes of Speke, Burton, Stanley and Livingstone, albeit in more modern gear and with more effective infrastructure.

We arrived midday in Dar, the first leg of our trip. It was a two-hour flight, enough time for each of us to get enthusiastic about the upcoming trip. Getting into Tanzania was a breeze as we all had East African visas. We did not book a hotel in advance, mostly because of cost, so our first order of business was to find a place to stay in Dar. The first day of our adventure was before us.

Eight of us jumped into a couple cabs from the airport to find a place to sleep in Dar. Given our limited funds, and knowing it was only the first day of a long trip, we avoided the larger hotels and sought more modest accommodation. Very modest as it turned out. One of our drivers suggested that we stay at the Florida Inn, which was on a small, cluttered road in the heart of Dar. When we got to the hotel, we were advised that the hotel had only one room available, and this lonely room had only one bed. So, we quickly slipped into Peace Corps mode and found a simple solution. Eight of us took the room, at a total cost of Tanzania Shillings fifteen (at that time, about $2) per night. We stayed for one night. I can't remember the sleeping arrangements -- perhaps it is best that I don't!

We spent the rest of the day in Dar, enjoying the sights and sounds of that nation's capital. The plaza in front of the New Africa Hotel was the central meeting place for all international visitors. We headed there, had something to drink and talked to all and sundry in the plaza. This was the biggest city that any of us had been in since we left Nairobi at the end of the last year. There were crowds of people, cars, curbside stores and vendors. This was raw, urban Africa. With its colours, music, noise, smells, sights, sounds. A carnival of the exotic for the uninitiated. For the villagers that we had each become, we revelled in it.

The next morning, we started our journey to Moshi, the town closest to Mt. Kilimanjaro. But not as planned. We had expected to take the train that day from Dar to Moshi, the city which housed the hotel from which we would start our climb. But our luck ran out immediately. Due to heavy flooding the previous few days, the train was unable to make the journey. We immediately huddled and found the perfect solution for cash poor, adventure rich Peace Corps Volunteers. We would hitchhike our way to Moshi.

To increase our chances of getting to Moshi on time, we split into smaller groups, with the requirement that we all had to be at the Marangu Hotel in Moshi no later than the night of December 17th, as the climb would begin the morning of December 18th. Three other Volunteers, Dave, Pete and Joe joined me as we attempted to hitchhike to Moshi from Dar. Even four people was too large to convince drivers to stop. We eventually split into two groups to make it easier to catch rides. Pete and I took seven short rides and only got about 100 kilometers from Dar in a few hours. We were standing on a lonely road, hundreds of kilometers from Moshi, when a bus came by with the word “Moshi” written on its headboard. We stopped the bus, hopped on and rode the rest of the way in "bus luxury", sharing the bus with people traveling with their goats, chickens and infant babies, mewling and puking in their arms. The bus was a local, stopping frequently at bus stops and anywhere else that a fare could be collected. After hours and hours of stopping and starting, we finally arrived in Moshi, exhausted.

We eventually found our way to the Marangu Hotel where we had reserved rooms for the night of December 17th. The hotel is located at the base of Mt. Kilimanjaro, in full view of its majestic and mighty magnificence. The Marangu Hotel was the starting point for our five-day climb. It is a hotel in the mold of the Norfolk Hotel in Nairobi, folksy, rural, traditional, one level, with a main block of rooms together and several little chalets spotted around the grounds of the hotel. It was clean and had beds for each of us. Most luxurious after a night at the Florida Inn. I had a room in the main hotel block, and was so tired that I cannot remember whom I shared a room with. It was much more expensive than the Florida Inn, with a nightly fare of forty Tanzania shillings a night, around $5.75.

We met for breakfast the next day in the sunshine of a bright Tanzanian morning, a good omen at the start of our climb. Several of us were very tired from the long and disjointed trip from Dar to Moshi. But a good cuppa, tea or coffee, and some tasty bacon and eggs re-energized each of us. We shared lots of hand shaking, back slapping (no high fives in those days) and smart-ass comments about our abilities to get to the top. Our climbing group comprised ten Peace Corps Volunteers from Malawi: Dave, Harold, Joe, Pete C, Pete W, Steve, Walt, and myself; Jack and Bill joined from another route. We were all men, plus one Peace Corps Volunteer from Botswana, a Swedish woman named Ingrid (whom I still remember as German) and an equal number of porters, carrying our food and equipment. Most of the porters were from the local Chagga tribe. After the usual running about like cats amok, we were prepared for our first steps from our homespun, rural hotel to the top of Africa.

Most of us were outfitted in familiar khaki shorts (though I started in Bermudas), shirts, climbing shoes or sneakers and a wooden walking stick with a pointed metal end. Most important of all, we each had slung over one shoulder or the other the requisite camera. We may not have needed the walking stick, but it made us each look like serious climbers. Each of us also brought with us, carried by the porters, a backpack with other clothes, toiletries and books to read. Given the technology of the times, we were more into each other than into ear-plugged worlds of music and podcasts (a word which didn't then exist). We left before lunch, and began the long trudge up the mountain, in unison, in good spirits, and with the freedom of not having any responsibility in the world. Freedom to climb, freedom to relax, freedom to share, freedom in the deepest meaning of the word.

On Day 1, our objective was Mandara Hut, which is located at an altitude of 2,700 metres, just below 9,000 feet. Mandara Hut is set at the base of the Rongai Forest (a wet, almost rainforest-like area). The climb from the Marangu Hotel took us about three hours. We meandered along a dirt road, which passed through a series of coffee plantations, consisting of orderly rows of glimmering, green-leafed bushes. The beans were yet to begin their march to maturity. The weather was sunny, our spirits were buoyant. A feeling of camaraderie permeated our group of intrepid climbers. As we walked, we joked, told stories, reminisced about Peace Corps training and our first year in Malawi; in fact, we continued the sharing process that was characteristic of our group from the beginning. Needless to say, we were happy campers.

We arrived at Mandara Hut in the late afternoon. The hut was a wooden cabin with bunks for over 20 persons to sleep. We sat outside the cabin, drinking in both the view and the beer which had been carried up the mountain for us. Already the temperature felt cooler. After finding our individual backpacks, we changed into warmer clothes. In the darkness of early evening, our porters began to prepare our dinners. It took us little time to devour a hot meal and put more beer in our bellies. After we ate, we sat around, singing Christmas songs and chatting in the same way good friends around the world confirm their friendships. We hadn't walked too far, and we weren't too tired. But an early night to bed was in order. I found it a bit hard to get to sleep, as I had developed a cough as soon as I reached Mandara Hut. Little did I know at that time what fate had in store for me.

The next morning, after breakfast, we were ready to climb through the Rongai Rain Forest on our way to the second cabin, Horombo Hut which is located at 3,720 metres, about 12,275 feet. The rainforest began only a few steps from our base at Mandara Hut. Immediately upon entering the Rongai Rain Forest, we felt cold and damp. We were constantly walking upwards in muddy and slippery circumstances. In fact we slid more than walked our way upwards. It was hard to reconcile the conditions in the rainforest with our former experiences of dry, African heat. Each rainforest has its own character and this one was no different. The canopy above reduced the amount of light in the rainforest. Yet all was green and lush. Because we were walking constantly upwards, the efforts we made produced lots of sweat in a damp and cold environment. My cough festered and continued to develop in these conditions.

The trip through the rainforest seemed a long one. Likely the trek was only an hour or so. As we emerged from the rainforest into the bright African sun, we had an excellent view of Mawenzi Peak (which is at 4,330 metres, about 14,300 feet), the second tallest of the three cones of Mt. Kilimanjaro. A horrific story was taking place there, but we didn't learn of this until we got to Horombo Hut. Instead, we walked across the open savannah or moorland in warm sunshine, continuing the happy jaunt we made from the Marangu Hotel to Mandara Hut, constantly going upwards and upwards. The second day's trek took about five hours. With Peace Corps enthusiasm in abundance, we experienced an appreciation of the unique environment in front of us on the slopes of Mt. Kilimanjaro and a celebration of our friendships which had blossomed over the past fifteen months.

Horombo Hut is located at the end of the so-called Kikelewa moorland. While we weren't exhausted, it was still heart-warming to get to our accommodations for the second night. An evening of tasty and warm food, and raucous singing of Christmas carols and other odds and sods had us in great spirits. Sadly for me, my cough continued and interrupted my sleep throughout the night.

It was also at this point that we learned about the tragedy that had occurred on Mt. Mawenzi while we were climbing. Two experienced climbers who had left some days before we started our climb were attempting to climb Mt. Mawenzi. Theirs was a real climb, requiring pitons, hammers, ropes and all the usual gear for a mountain assault. The two men had "gone missing", and a search for them had begun as we had started our climb.

I'm not sure if we heard this through the bush telegraph (our porters) or whether another source was involved. Once we were ensconced in Horombo Hut, we were told that two climbers had slipped while climbing the peak, and had fallen but only to the extent of the ropes which secured them, a distance of a hundred feet. Unfortunately, they had been unable to climb back up the ropes, and eventually died hanging at the end of their tethered existence. The contrast between their serious attempt to climb Mt. Mawenzi and our "walk in the park" Kibo cone of Mt. Kilimanjaro climb couldn't have been starker.

The next morning, we began the third day of our climb. This was to be the day of another, long five hour walk. As we left Horombo Hut, we immediately started across the so-called "saddle", which is an open desert, with very little vegetation other than scrub grass and rocks everywhere. It is dominated by a sandy colour, strong cross winds and a bleak and stark countenance. The object of this day's climb was to reach by late afternoon the third hut which is called Kibo Hut; it sits at 4,703 metres, or about 15,520 feet. From Kibo Hut, the route goes to Gilman's Point, at the edge of the Kibo crater. The highest point along the crater is Uhuru Peak, located at 5,895 metres, or 19,341 feet.

Ten miles and five hours later, we achieved our goal and found ourselves at Kibo Hut in the late afternoon. We all looked a bit haggard from the endless walking and the thinner air at a higher altitude. We sat outside the Hut and talked about the success of the first three days and the prospects for the upcoming climb that night. In the early evening we ate a hot meal, and tried to get to sleep right after dinner. We were to begin the last leg of the climb just after midnight. As I lay down and tried to sleep, I continued the cough which I evidenced the entire day of the third leg.

The porters awakened us around midnight. Most of us didn't sleep well. I was tired and still had a persistent, hacking cough. Nevertheless, we each got warmly dressed and then left the hut. I immediately found the going slow and ponderous. We began walking up through the scree that covered the mountain. Three steps up, then a two step slide back. After a several minutes of trying to manage the scree, I found it impossible to breathe which made it even more difficult to walk. One of the porters walked with me. Slowly. He wouldn't leave my side. Most of my colleagues were ahead of me and kept getting further ahead. At about 1,000 feet above the hut, after maybe one hour of walking and sliding and walking and sliding, despite my best efforts, I could not take another step. I couldn't breathe. I was exhausted. One of the guys never left Kibo Hut. He gave up on the last leg before it started. Of the group that continued the climb, I was the only one who eventually had to stop and return. Beaten, battered and unsuccessful. Tired from my endless coughing, unable to breathe easily, and finding every step to be difficult, nay impossible, I had no choice but to return to Kibo Hut. Instead of heading to the peak and endless photo ops with my close friends, I was led by my guide back down the mountain to Kibo Hut.

Arriving at the Hut, I sat down, disappointed, dejected and dazed, and awaited the return of the successful climbers (including that darn Swedish/German woman walking machine). It was still early in the morning, long before the rising sun would brighten the day. Perhaps the darkness of the night only emphasized my failure to reach the peak. Mt. Kilimanjaro had conquered me, had beaten me down. I coughed my way through the rest of the night, unable to sleep again, shivering and waiting for my friends. It took forever before I heard their shouts and joyous exaltations. While I was excited for them, I was once again upset that I couldn't reach the top.

After we collected all our belongings, we started back down to Horombo Hut, the second hut, where we would spend the fourth night. As indicated above, I could not walk at all. I was tired and coughing. So, one of porters, who was at least six feet four inches tall, placed very sick me on his shoulders and ran back for ten miles down to Horombo Hut. I felt time and again that I would fall off. Pete C ran alongside me and my saviour. We had to stop from time to time so the porter could rest -- but to be honest, so I could rest too. I continued coughing, held the porter's head tightly as he ran, and tried to make sure I didn't lean one way or the other, which would cause us both to fall.

That night at Horombo Hut was turbulent. I couldn't sleep, I was still coughing and I felt tired and miserable. This contrasted with the ebullient enjoyment of my colleagues who had made it to the top. They had stories aplenty, beer even more plenty, and would they have had iPhones, there would have been more photos than stories.

The next morning, which was the fifth day of the climb, my porter saviour and I started our symbiotic relationship again. Once I was on his shoulders again, the run began. For the ten mile run though the open veld, this was harrowing enough. Rest stops along the way kept me sane. The pressure of holding the head of the porter and trying to maintain my balance as he ran tried my physical capabilities. When we got to the top of the Rongai Rain Forest, with about an hour to go, the porter continued our downward trend, he with me on his shoulders, running through wet and slippery mud, low branches and other hazards. I have no idea how we made it through the rainforest and back to Mandara Hut without me falling off. I have photos of my travails on the shoulders of a porter, but these are stored in the Alpharetta, Georgia warehouse where many of my photos of Africa (and beyond) are sleeping, even today.

We stopped briefly at Mandara Hut before we continued the final ten miles of the trip back to the Marangu Hotel. This part of the trip had a more gentle slope, back though coffee plantations on a solid dirt road. As we got to a lower altitude, I was able to give up my porter ride, and walk the rest of the way. It wasn't easy, and I was exhausted from little sleep and endless coughing. But my ability to balance on the shoulders of any person was at wit's end. So walk I did.

At the bottom of the mountain, I was sick as a dog and needed treatment. The Marangu Hotel recommended that I see an old British doctor, who had lived in the area for donkey's years. He was in his 60s, which seemed really old to me, and was eccentric to the extreme. Almost a caricature of an old British doctor in not so urban Africa. William Boyd-esque. It didn't take Mr. Brit Doctor long to determine the cause of my cough and frailty. He whipped out his stethoscope, asked me to breathe in and out (which was challenging enough) and announced with the certainly of a man who has seen it all that I had double pneumonia, or "walking pneumonia". While the doctor's name is lost in time, I do remember the equipment he used to treat me. He gave me a large injection of penicillin, with a long needle connected to a hard, rubbery syringe, that twisted and turned in his hand as he loaded the penicillin. I have no idea how he got all the penicillin into my backside with the syringe bending this way and that. But he did.

The next dilemma was what to do with me. All of my Peace Corps friends were about to head on to other adventures, with Uganda as the target of the next phase of their travels. I had little money and no ability to afford a hotel. Recovery would take at least a week. Mr Brit

Doctor got in touch with someone in Moshi in the Peace Corps (since he learned that I was in the Peace Corps too). This unknown Peace Corps benefactor recommended that I stay with a local couple called the Armstrongs. That stay in Moshi was almost as interesting as the first part of this story.

I have no idea why I remember the surname of the Armstrongs. The husband was English; the wife was German. This was 1967 and they had married more than 20 years before, maybe even during World War II. An English – German marriage during the World War? Probably because they met in Tanzania and were not "enemies" as they would have been in Europe. I had just had a major jab in my backside so I wasn't totally with it when I arrived at their apartment. I was thankful that some kind people had agreed to let me live with them until I could get back on my feet.

As luck would have it, the German wife was a physiotherapist. Perfect for a double pneumonia victim. Twice a day, while I gorged on their food and hospitality, she would massage my chest and back. Each session involved at least 45 minutes of intensive pushing and pulling and pressuring and manipulating. I also took other dawa (medicine) which Mr Brit Doc had prescribed for me. In my mind, my speedy recovery was certainly helped along by her kind and strong German hands.

There wasn't much else to do during those Armstrong days. There were no televisions and the internet wasn't even a word. I had my own bedroom which allowed me to sleep peacefully regardless what was happening elsewhere in the apartment. As with most expatriates in Africa, the Armstrongs had an extensive library, much of it comprised of tomes on African subjects. Both fiction and non-fiction. When I wasn't being manhandled (or more accurately, woman handled) by Mrs. Armstrong, I had the run of the library. That was diversion number one. Diversion number two was a great and delightful surprise.

As part of the hospitality I experienced in Chez Armstrong that week was the presence and attention of their lovely daughter, Janet. She must have been around 20 years old. Bright, perky and very pretty with straight cut bangs above her eyes. I don't know if this is the treatment which Mr. Brit Doctor envisaged when he forced me to stay in Moshi for a week but it was definitely rehabilitating. My treatment consisted of being massaged twice a day by a German expert physio lady, fed by a British-German War couple and emotionally rehabilitated by spending time and talking frequently to Janet during my week of incarceration. What a great holiday this was turning out to be (even though I had no photos of myself at the top of Kilimanjaro)!! It was one I didn't want to share with my Peace Corps colleagues.

A week later, after sating myself with the aroma and hug-feeling environment of the Armstrong household, I sadly left Moshi. While I was recovering my health in such comfortable circumstances, I also knew that I had to leave and find the rest of my Peace Corps adventurers. That week in Moshi was triggered by my sudden and unexpected illness, but was not meant to replace the plans which my other Peace Corps buddies and I had made for half a year. Walking out of the comfort of their apartment was difficult, especially saying goodbye to Janet (there's a future in that story), no less than the trip to Kampala would be. I said my goodbyes, with a tear in my eye, and headed to a road which would lead me to the next phase of my school holiday.

I remember walking to a roadside, standing alone on the shoulder of a ubiquitous African dirt road, in an unfamiliar country, and waving my hand up and down at the cars that flew by. I was hitching to Nairobi on the first leg of my attempt to meet up with my Peace Corps gang in Kampala. They had stuck to their travel plans; I didn't want to delay any longer in joining them as we had long planned this holiday together. I wanted to be part of the story which we would tell our unborn children in the decades ahead.

The first ride of many was in a small truck. I was offered a seat on some katundu (luggage) outside in the back along with some other hitchhikers. I was asked in Swahili, "wewe nakwenda wapi" (where are you going?). I didn't know any Swahili but instinctively replied "nakwenda Nairobi" (going to Nairobi). They were satisfied, I was stunned at my linguistic effort and the truck pulled away. The next leg of my holiday in East Africa had begun.

All my other Malawi based-Volunteer friends had gone to Uganda through Mwanza, Tanzania and had taken the boat across Lake Victoria to reach Uganda. I wasn't as adventurous and didn't want to take a route through so many unknown places alone. My simple plan was to hitchhike north to Nairobi, Kenya, spend a night there, hang a left to the West, and continue hitching until I got to Kampala. That was the plan. And that is in fact what happened. My solo safari took two and a half days to get from the quiet of a Moshi-based life to the hustle and bustle of the largest city in Uganda. Arriving just before the New Year, the start of 1968, I hooked up with my Peace Corps friends and continued with the planned holiday.

There are two great stories which emerged after my arrival in Kampala. First was the next phase of my East African trip which I shared with Pete C. He had been living in Kamwendo, a small village near Mchinji, Malawi. The adventures of Pete and Jim are sufficiently unusual and interesting to form the basis of another story, soon to be recounted for our progeny. The second great story, which to date has never been told, whispered or otherwise revealed, was my reconnection with Janet of Armstrong fame in London in November 1968. This story too will finally be told. Both of these stories emerge from and are part of our Kilimanjaro climb, the adventure of a lifetime.

Sadly, because of my double pneumonia condition, I become a KiliFailure. I am one of the many climbers over endless years who have yearned to stand on the edge of the highest mountain in Africa and watch the sunrise from a point on the earth closer to the sun than most of us would ever have a chance to do again. That I never stood in those steps is in fact not so bad, as those who made it to the top have told their stories and shared their photos with me and others many times since their ascent and descent on that December 1967 day. The real triumph of the Kilimanjaro climb was the sharing of the planning and execution of the adventure with a group of people who have been an intimate part of my life since those glorious days of the late 1960s. It is that friendship which I celebrate even as a KiliFailure.

Completed: August 20, 2020

THE MALAWI SPORTS SCENE IN 1967 AND 1968

My Sporting Youth

Thwak. Serve. Thwak. Return. Thwak. Cross court. Thwak. Cross court. Thwak. Down the line. Winner! Cheers! A short tennis rally in words, ending with the sound of the crowd. I love this sport. Not being very tall, not being very fast, not being very strong, tennis to me was an equalizer. I found early on that, playing tennis, I could compete with taller, faster or stronger athletes than I was.

Like most young boys, I was a doer. A player. An active participant. I played all the sports that American boys played in the 1950s. My parents outplaced me to summer camp in Wisconsin from the ages of 10 to 15. Eight weeks every summer. To a camp that emphasized summer sports: baseball, basketball, swimming, archery, track and field and tennis. The magic of tennis.

I continued my fascination with tennis through high school and beyond. I was a starter on the New Trier boys' varsity tennis team, under the leadership of Coach Hugh Davis, a southerner with an accent unheard in Winnetka, Illinois. With my partner, Dick Avery, we won the regional high school doubles event in 1959 in my senior year at New Trier. Never forgot the headline on the back page of the *New Trier News* after that victory: "Friedlander, Avery Win Regional Doubles Tournament". Recognition. A Warhol moment.

My racket skills also drifted into badminton during those halcyon high school days. In my senior year, I won the boys' tournament for the entire school. Badminton Jim!!

At the University of Wisconsin, I was on the men's tennis team as a freshman. I also joined the AEPi fraternity and participated in every sport possible. At the annual AEPi awards dinner at the end of my freshman year, I was given the Best Athlete of AEPi award, in a year that Marty Stillman, an AEPi senior, was the best pitcher on the baseball team and one of the best pitchers in the Big Ten. I was given the award of Best Athlete of AEPi three of my four years at university. Maybe that's more a comment on AEPi than on myself.

In addition to my active life as an athlete at Wisconsin, I also was given my first opportunity at university to be involved in sports organization. In my senior year, 1962/63, I was employed by the university (at the then standard salary of $1 per hour) to assist ice hockey Coach Art Thomsen in organizing and managing the intra-mural sports program for the entire university. This covered all sports, for men and women, and all competitions from leagues to tournaments. The office I worked in was located inside the renowned Red Gym, where I had undergone mandatory swimming trials in 1959 as a freshman. The Red Gym still exists, without

Art or myself, sitting on the edge of the newly built Alumni Park.

The intra-mural sports program was designed and managed by Coach Art and myself. There were no computers, no photocopiers, no equipment of any type that would assist us in making this large and complicated program for all of the 15,000 undergraduates who wished to participate. We used pencil and paper to plan all the games and tournaments. And it worked. A lost art.

I attended Harvard Law School from September 1963 to May 1966. In the summers of 1964 and 1965, I did not follow the usual trek to internships at large law firms, which were prospective employers after graduation. Instead, I was hired by Middlefork Tennis Club, a small, local club in Northfield, Illinois, as the tennis pro. This was thanks to my good friend Wally Eiseman (later Dr. Wally) whose family was a member of the club. In 1965, while I was working at Middlefork, I became one of the original members of the then Professional Tennis Registry, the first attempt to organize tennis professionals in the United States.

Peace Corps Training, Syracuse, New York

After graduation from Harvard Law School in June 1966, I joined the US Peace Corps. The excitement of the first couple weeks of Peace Corps training at Syracuse University began in September 1966. We trained for twelve weeks to be secondary school teachers in the southeastern African country of Malawi. We were offered instruction about Malawi and its geography, history, language, sociology and culture. Sensitivities were sinisterly discussed in hushed tones when the President's name was mentioned. This was our first warning about Malawi's President, Dr. Hastings Kamuzu Banda, and his lack of a sense of humor and concern about how Peace Corps Volunteers dressed when working in Malawi. We began our language immersion in Chinyanja, taught by able trio of Aloysius Dziko, John Chimgoga and Malon Chidzungu.

The Peace Corps Director in Malawi, Will Lotter, came back to the US to visit all twenty-six of us at the beginning of our training program. We were known in Peace Corps parlance as Malawi X, the tenth Peace Corps group to be sent to Malawi (the first was sent in 1963). Lotter's attendance at training was *de rigueur* for all Peace Corps programs, making the organization more personal with close interaction between Volunteers and staff in country. During Will's visit, we had preliminary discussions about our likely teaching assignments in Malawi, though no commitments were made early on.

Will also mentioned that there might be a sports organizer position available if any of us might be more interested in teaching and organizing sports than teaching in a classroom. Steve, Larry and I (all lawyers by the way) each affirmed our interest in the sports organizer position. No decision was taken at that time, but I felt that my foot was in the door even if I had no control of what would happen in Malawi. Any talk about sports organization was forgotten during the rest of training in Syracuse.

Full Time Teaching; Part Time Sporting

Why have I focused on my early sporting life? To provide a reason for my interest in being a sports organizer as a Peace Corps Volunteer in Malawi. When I joined the Peace Corps, I was offered and accepted a position as a secondary school English teacher. I only learned where I would be posted after I arrived in Malawi when each of us was told by Peace Corps staff where we would be teaching. My assignment was Henry Henderson Institute (HHI), the largest non-boarding secondary school in Blantyre, the biggest city in Malawi. My first obligation was to teach English to students who were in the last year of secondary school, in preparation for the dreaded Cambridge exam. This I began to do at the end of January 1967 when school opened after the holidays.

Upon arrival at HHI, I found three other Volunteers from the Malawi VIII contingent already teaching there. They had been at HHI for a year. I ended up rooming with one of them, John Geraghty, a history teacher. The other two Volunteers were Arlee May, who taught math and science and Sandy Laufer who taught English for classes before the last year of secondary school.

Will Lotter was the consummate Peace Corps Director. Gregarious and athletic, he was also an enthusiastic tennis player. Will had been in Malawi over eighteen months when our Malawi X contingent arrived. During this time, he started playing (and training) Malawi's premier young tennis player, Bwanali K. Maluwa ("flower" in Chinyanja).

Maluwa was in his last year of secondary school when I started teaching at HHI. After Will introduced me to Maluwa, I took over as his tennis coach. I began to play with and teach Maluwa several times a week. Maluwa was better with his forehand and backhand than with his spelling and writing. Not a classroom star. But tennis became the basis of our lifelong friendship until he passed away from AIDS in the early 1990s.

Testing the Sporting Waters

For the first two terms of the 1967 secondary school year (Malawi was on an annual school year), I was a diligent and committed English teacher and personal coach of Malawi's number one tennis player. These time commitments changed when Ray Batchelor was appointed Malawi's Director of Sport in July 1967.

Ray was an Englishman who had been in Kenya for the previous two years where he had served as Director of Sport. As a teenager, he had played football on West Ham's junior team. He never made it to the first side at West Ham. He later attended Loughborough College in England to obtain his qualifications as a coach in various sports. His daughter, Claire, had won the Kenya National Women's Tennis title at the age of 15 in 1966. The family's arrival in Malawi in July 1967 changed my life and work as a Peace Corps Volunteer.

Within a month of Batchelor's arrival in Malawi, together we began to establish a youth sports centre unique in Malawi. The headquarters of this new sports centre was a hectare of land across the road from the Queen Elizabeth Hospital in Blantyre. The land was donated to the Government of Malawi by the Lions Club. The Lions Club is an international organization which was established in Chicago, Illinois back in 1917. Its simple and direct mission is: We Serve! Its clubs are places where individuals join together to give their valuable time and effort to improving their local communities, and the world.

The fenced plot of land given to the Government of Malawi included a football pitch, two cement tennis courts, without nets, and a changing room/toilet block for boys and girls. There was also an area where a netball pitch was later added, along with a volleyball court and a basketball court. The red bricked Queen Elizabeth Hospital building was across the street, a stone's throw away, hovering above the new sports ground. In 1968, I convinced the Lions Club to build a wall by the court for tennis practice and to provide tarps for the court fencing to cut down the wind. The facilities started to look more professional as time went on.

The Blantyre Youth Sports Centre (BYSC)

Batchelor wanted to use this plot of land mainly for developing young footballers in the Blantyre area. I wanted to use the tennis courts for developing Malawi's future tennis champions. We decided to do both through the formation of a club, which we named prosaically the Blantyre Youth Sports Centre (BYSC). There was no model for the structure of the BYSC. It is worth describing this club to show how special it was.

The basis of the BYSC was the two football leagues that would play on the pitch at the sports ground: boys 18 and under, and boys 14 and under. The members of the BYSC had to be from primary schools only, as secondary schools had their own sports facilities. This club was for the disenfranchised. Within six weeks of announcing the start of the club, we had formed thirty teams of sixteen players each in the 18 and under league and eighteen teams of sixteen players each in the 14 and under league. Over 700 young boys.

Each member of the BYSC had to pay a tiki (3 pence) a year in membership dues (and if they couldn't afford it, Batchelor and I would quietly cover the cost). We wanted each new member to understand that these facilities were not free. We wanted them to use the facilities, and to care for them. To assist Batchelor and me in supervising and manging the BYSC, we set up an advisory group with representatives from six age groups: 7-8 year olds, 9-10 year olds, 11-12 year-olds, etc up to 17-18 year olds. These six representatives met with Batchelor and me from time to time to discuss the way the club was managed, and to voice complaints and suggestions from their respective age groups. This organization was to become even more important in the next couple years, when we expanded the fixed assets at the BYSC; but that's a later story.

The football leagues were an immediate success. Some of the teams approached private companies for sports kit with adverts. Others were as ragtag as would be expected. We prepared a schedule of games, using the sports organizational skills I developed at the University of Wisconsin. We trained men and senior boys to be referees for the scheduled games. The results were posted each week on a signboard at the changing room block. The competition was on; it was fierce.

On the tennis side, I was able to find an initial group of about a dozen young boys, from the ages of eight to sixteen, who professed an interest in learning how to play tennis. We had no tennis nets and no tennis rackets and no tennis balls. which made teaching tennis a challenge. To begin to get around these slight difficulties, I went to a sports store and begged for them to provide us with two tennis nets.

Surprisingly they did. To solve our lack of rackets problem, I bought a plywood board four feet by eight feet by ¾ inch. I designed a small paddle about eighteen inches in length, and had fifteen paddles cut from the plywood board. These were the first "rackets" for the soon to be Malawi tennis champions at BYSC.

During the six-month period after I brought the paddles to the club and made them available to the first tennis students, I made the new-to-tennis youngsters play only with the paddles. Maluwa joined me in teaching the youngsters. He brought credibility to our effort, as he was already the best tennis player in Malawi. In addition, he played on the Malawi national football team. He was admired and respected by all the prospective tennis champions in my bailiwick.

To be effective, I had to learn to teach tennis in Chinyanja. Using about ten helpful phrases, I was able to accomplish this quickly. At the end of six months, I selected the top four players who had been using paddles and allowed them to use the four tennis rackets which had been donated to the club earlier. We also begged embassies, businesses and sports clubs for tennis balls. Rarely did we have new balls; if it bounced, we were glad to have it. My biggest surprise was to see how proficient these youngsters were playing tennis with these short, plywood paddles, hitting soft, oft mishappen balls.

Sports beyond BYSC

In addition to my work with the BYSC, Batchelor asked me to take an active role in the administration of sport in the country. Between September 1967 and March 1968, I became the first Hon. Secretary of each of the following new sporting bodies in Malawi: the Amateur Athletic Association of Malawi, the Amateur Boxing Association of Malawi and the Olympic and Commonwealth Games Association of Malawi. Most of these secretarial positions involved paperwork, writing letters to the international headquarters of each of these associations and attending (and taking minutes at) meetings of these sports associations in Malawi.

The only risky position was the one in the Amateur Boxing Association, not because I was Hon. Secretary but because the Association appointed me official Timekeeper at all their boxing events. There was little risk that I would enter the ring when any boxer was there; I would have been knocked out by the first whish of air that came my way. The danger of being Timekeeper was that I had to sit next to the ring when performing my timekeeping role. As such, when one boxer was pummelling another boxer, drawing blood in many cases, all of us at the officials table next to the ring were in the "circle of blood splatter" that would come from many of the punches. I never attended a boxing match at this time without getting blood on me. This was long before HIV/AIDS reared its ugly head.

In addition, Batchelor wanted me to become proficient as a referee in all athletics (track and field) events. I became the first official Starter (yes, with a gun--shooting blanks thankfully) of regional and national athletics competitions. He made me take exams in every field event. By the summer of 1968, I had qualified to be an official for all track and field events (excluding the hammer throw; we didn't have the equipment to protect other athletes and officials from the random execution of this event by less experienced athletes). Most events were a joy to officiate as there was little danger to myself or other officials or athletes. This was less true in the javelin event, which allowed unskilled athletes to hurl a long, pointed pole as far as they could, more or less in the direction of where measurements were made. I remember more than one wayward throw which led to the scattering of all those in the range of the javelin as it hurled into the sky toward whomever it wanted to find. Fortunately, no injuries from a javelin took place during the athletics events of 1967 and 1968.

The Army and the Police in Athletics

As part of my initial responsibilities as a sports organizer in 1967, I spent a lot of time with the soldiers in the Malawi Army and the policemen in the Malawi Police. Both organizations, in addition to their main duties of protecting the citizens of the realm, were very active in sports competitions; a good way to bond as teammates and colleagues. At all athletics competitions, the Malawi Army and the Malawi Police were the largest teams participating. They also held their own internal competitions at their various sports facilities.

I became friendly with the leaders of these two security organizations while I was a sports organizer. The Malawi Army was headed by bushy-moustached Brigadier Paul Lewis (who was Colonel Lewis when I first met him) and the Malawi Police by Commissioner Peter Long. Both were very experienced in their areas of responsibility with long careers before coming to Malawi. Similar in stature, they were tall, ample, larger than life, enormous presences in their respective institutions. Not surprisingly, both were from the UK. Although they had to work together in their jobs, they were extremely competitive when it came to sports. When one or the other's team had a better record in an athletics meeting or a cross country event, their respective chests expanded to the full extent of their impressive uniforms.

While helping to organise athletics competitions, I became very friendly with the captains of the Army and Police athletics teams. First was Capt. Buxton Namwali, a baby-faced soldier. His Army teams were always fit and competitive. On the Police side, the captain was Barry Thorne, a young roustabout who made training and competition fun. Barry was never at a loss for jokes or smiles. This did not make him any less competitive but helped to make coaching and competing a joy.

Motorcycle Misery

From the middle of 1967, I had many balls in the air at the same time; not just tennis balls. My primary job was as a secondary school English teacher at HHI preparing sixty students (in two levels) for the Cambridge exams at the end of the year. I was active as a sports organizer with the Director of Sports, managing the BYSC and coaching Maluwa on a weekly basis. To help me get around, the Peace Corps office approved my having a motorcycle (which was denied to all other teachers in the country). I was given a Yamaha 125, the first motorcycle I ever rode in my life. It was maintained at the Peace Corps motor pool by Ali Waka and his team. Ali eventually became a close friend after my marriage to one of his relatives in Malawi.

It didn't take long for me to have my first (and only) accident in Malawi with my beloved motorcycle. Given the number of miles I travelled in the Southern Region of Malawi over the next eighteen months, this was a miracle. The accident is burned into my memory (as it was into my hands). It happened within the first week that I had the motorcycle.

I was traveling from the school, HHI, back into the centre of town. Less than a mile away. Fortunately, I was going at a modest speed, probably no more than fifteen miles per hour. When I reached the main bus stop in Blantyre, which was to my right, I started down a steep hill toward the Blantyre Clock Tower at the bottom. Without warning, a cyclist on my left made a ninety-degree turn just as I was passing by. He turned right into the front of the motorcycle. My unfamiliarity with the motorcycle's various gadgets meant that I didn't hit the brake and stop; I stopped by hitting the bicycle and falling down to my right, with the motorcycle on top of me. The engine was still running; and I was totally disoriented. I knew I had to get the motorcycle off me. Without any experience with motorcycles, I put my hands on the exhaust pipe to lift the motorcycle from resting on me. Not the most intelligent move I ever made – anywhere. The heat of the exhaust pipe burned my hands immediately; I screamed. The cyclist never heard my primal cry as he ran away as soon as I ran my motorcycle into him and his bicycle.

Result? I had injuries on my elbows, knees and legs which required treatment and bandaging. And of course, my burnt hands, which were encased in bandages after being treated with various ointments and medicines to ease the pain and start the healing process. Somewhere in my many thousands of photos of Malawi is a black and white photo of myself, bandaged all over my body and standing shorts with neither smile nor understanding. The motorcycle also suffered injuries, but replacing motorcycle parts I discovered is easier than replacing hands, arms and legs.

My Friend Harold

During the rest of 1967, I shared my sports organization role with Harold Salmon, the Volunteer who had been a full-time sports organizer since January 1966 when he arrived in the country. Harold was a Bobby Hull lookalike. He had a beaming smile, and a warm personality to match. He was open and engaging with everyone he met. Harold was not a fluent speaker of Chinyanja. He knew about seven words, but he used them well and often. He was so convincing that when he left Malawi in December 1967 to return to the US, the sports writer on the *The Times*, Levson Lifikilo, noted that Harold was an outstanding sports organizer and a friend to all Malawians, largely due to his fluency in Chinyanja. Harold must have said zikomo (thank you), zikomo zikomo (his favorite set of words) to Levson as he departed from Chileka Airport.

Central Stadium

When I first arrived in Malawi in 1967, the national athletics competition was traditionally held each year at Central Stadium, which itself had and has had an adventure in the world of names. Originally named Rangeley Stadium after a British civil servant in Nyasaland, Malawi's colonial name, its Central Stadium moniker was lost in 1968 when the seating was expanded to 65,000 and the name changed, not unexpectedly, to Kamuzu Stadium. From the mid-1960s until 1994, there were lots of Kamuzu thises and thats throughout Malawi. After Bakili Muluzu became President in 1994, the name was changed to Chichiri Stadium (where it is located). This only lasted until his successor, Bingu wa Mutharika, became President. In 2004, Bingu renamed it, once again, as Kamuzu Stadium.

When I first started organizing sports, I spent a lot of time at Central Stadium. It was managed by Mr. L Saidi, who had much experience in stadium management. Most important for the national and regional athletics competitions held there was the marking of the track. The surface of the track was a reddish coloured laterite clay called murram on which whitewash, consisting of lime and water, had to be laid as lines for lanes for the track events. Saidi was an expert at both the measurement of the width and direction of the lanes and application of the whitewash. It was a painstaking process, done by hand. Through Saidi, I learned the intricacy and difficulty of ensuring that a lane for a 400 metre event would actually be 400 metres long and that each lane had exactly the same width. In a world of laser measurement instruments, these skills are neither necessary nor appreciated.

Saidi became a close friend during my first year in Malawi. We often sat together at Central Stadium, taking a break, as he educated me about life's realities in Malawi. He helped me to understand the financial pressures on wage earners in urban Malawi. His salary was £35 a month (mine was £38 and I lived alone). Not only did he have to take care of his wife and several young kids who lived in Blantyre with him, he was also responsible for the school fees and other financial obligations of an endless stream of about thirty relatives back in his home village. He was constantly desperate about his lack of funds, which affected his ability to work. This situation was multiplied by the number of urban Malawians with poor, rural relatives whose hands were always in the pockets of the urbanites.

Professional Boxing in Malawi

From late September until the end of October 1967, at Batchelor's insistence, I got involved in the organization of a very special event: a professional boxing tournament. Perhaps Batchelor wanted to bring a spectacular boxing show to the Malawi people; perhaps he wanted to make money for the Department of Sport. But whatever his motive, Batchelor got in bed with some very dicey

Portuguese professional boxing promoters. The main event on a night of seven bouts was to be the middleweight clash between King Marshall Jetu, a Malawian living in South Africa, and the appropriately named John Fighter of Rhodesia. More on the match after I describe the way the deal was sealed.

One Sunday afternoon, Batchelor asked me to show up at Maxims, Blantyre's renowned Portuguese restaurant famous for its piri-piri dishes, mainly chicken and prawns. Batchelor told me to "dress up" as we were meeting important officials from the Mozambique boxing community. At this point in my life, I hadn't the vaguest idea how to organize a professional boxing match. Probably the same holds true today. I also didn't know how to dress up, other than to wear trousers and a white shirt.

At Maxims, we met with two very slick, oily, black-haired, fast-talking Portuguese professional boxing promoters. They had a "deal" for us. They would bring the "famous" Malawian boxer, King Marshall Jetu, back from South Africa to fight against the up and coming Rhodesian boxer named John Fighter. They said we would fill the stadium, meaning Central Stadium in Blantyre. This meant money for the Department of Sport.

On the afternoon of this Sunday meeting, in the darkened interior of Maxims, we were served the largest prawns I had ever seen. Each was bigger than a quarter pounder. The first dish put in the centre of the oil cloth covered table was more than a foot high, covered with giant piri piri prawns. There were so many in the pile that we each had six. Along with the endless large-sized and hot flavored giant prawns was a waterfall of beer from Mozambique, either Manica, Dos (two) M (MacMahan) or Laurentina. All were excellent beers and went down smoothly with the hot tasting giant prawns. We ate through the first foot of giant prawns, after which the owner of the restaurant, no doubt with a wad of bills tucked into his pocket from his Portuguese citizen boxing promoter buddies, brought out another foot of giant piri piri prawns. It was over this mass of giant prawns and endless beer that the deal was carved to bring professional boxing to Malawi for the first time. I felt pride in being part of history; my stomach felt otherwise.

The event took place at the end of October 1967. Thankfully my piri piri overkill at Maxims had subsided by the day of the fight. On a warm weekend afternoon, Central Stadium was filled with 20,000 Malawi citizens, screaming and shouting for their favourite boxers. The first six events were merely the appetizers for the main contest. When King Marshall Jetu entered the ring with his embossed, shiny and flowing robe, the crowd went ballistic. John Fighter entered the ring to a chorus of boos. Jetu was shorter, more compact, and not very fast moving. Fighter was taller, with a long arm reach, and a younger spring to his step. After the introductions by a professional referee brought into Malawi specifically for this event, the fighters returned to their corners and readied for the contest.

Because this was a professional bout, I wasn't asked to be the timekeeper. Thankfully. Instead, I spectated like the rest of the crowd. King Marshall Jetu plodded into the ring at the first bell, and joined combat with the taller, swifter fighter, Fighter. It was evident in the first round who the winner of the contest would be. But King Marshall Jetu, with 20,000 shouting voices in his corner, hung on until the fifth round, when he was unceremoniously knocked to the ground for good. The crowd which had expected so much of their champion was gutted. King Marshall Jetu looked gutted too. Professional boxing had come to Malawi. And my stomach prayed that no more professional fight negotiations would ever take place at Maxims.

Full Time Sports Organizer

After my return to Malawi in mid-January from my December Kilimanjaro climbing adventure with other Malawi Xers, I moved from the comfort of my two-bedroomed, red-bricked teacher's house at HHI to a smaller, one-bedroomed, whitewashed Ministry house near Kwacha National Culture Centre. Accompanying me to the Kwacha Centre house was houseboy George Amani, a black dog named Ujeni, the Peace Corps book locker, some clothes and my unnamed motorcycle. After organizing myself in my new abode near the not so challenging Mt. Soche (after Kilimanjaro, all Malawi "mountains" were foothills), I began my work as assistant to Batchelor on a full-time basis. I was even busier than during my school year at HHI.

In 1968 our work at the BYSC continued unabated. Football leagues were scheduled and managed, tennis teaching reached a crescendo, and even a netball league began. We visited the BYSC every week to help with its development and management. Fortunately, the offices of the Director of Sport were on the second floor of Mandala House, only a short motorcycle ride to the BYSC. We were a small team: Batchelor, myself and a couple support staff.

Mandala House was built in 1882 for the manager of the African Lakes Corporation. It is still an old colonial style, two story building, with a surrounding veranda, set in spacious gardens. Today it is the home to the Society of Malawi, the repository of all Malawi history and publishers of tracts on Malawi history. It used to be located on the Old Mandala Road, which road has now been renamed Kaohsiung Road. I won't even ask why.

Back to 1968. My tennis coaching took a new turn. I designed a way for kids to practice hitting a tennis ball by putting an elastic cord through a tennis ball and tying it to the ground and to a support about five feet off the ground. This gave the kids the ability to swing through the ball with a racket or a plywood paddle, on both the forehand and backhand sides.

We also decided to form a team to compete in the men's tennis league, which consisted mainly of teams from the exclusive clubs in Blantyre, Limbe and Zomba. Our home ground was at the BYSC. We called the team the Rackets Club (not the racquets club as might have been expected). The team was headed by George Martin, an American lawyer working as a legal advisor to the Malawi Government on a program from Syracuse University. George was the top player in the country, having won the National Men's championship in 1967. The rest of the Rackets Club were all young Malawians: Maluwa, Henry Juwa, Francis Mvula, Houston Nkunga, Edson Timba, Harvey Deleza and myself. Surprisingly, we were formidable though a new team to the men's tennis league. We were to play seven matches during the season and expected to win the league championship in our first year as a team. We didn't win the championship but sometimes it's the thought that counts.

Cross-country continued through March, with events at the Malawi Army in Zomba, Blantyre Secondary School, the Young Pioneers at Misomali and the

National Championships in April. We also organized a 10-mile road race from Chileka Airport straight into Blantyre. I watched and didn't participate.

In the spring, we established a Blantyre tennis league for all schools in Blantyre. For 14 and under and 18 and under. The BYSC boys outclassed the boarding school tennis players at every level, despite in some cases being ten years younger than their opponents. The success of our tennis efforts at BYSC was apparent to all.

On 21st April 1968, an international tennis match with Rhodesia was organized and took place at the Limbe Club. The visiting Rhodesian squad included powerhouses like Hank Irvine, Andrew Pattison, Des McKenzie and Sherry Towers. The Malawi team was headed by George Martin (US) and Alfeo Vatteroni (an Italian who was the manager of the Chiperoni Blanket Factory in Cholo), both former national men's champions. Maluwa and I played doubles against Towers and McKenzie. We lost in two hard fought sets. The expertise and experience of the Rhodesian players were displayed as the Malawi team, except for George, lost badly. It was the first and last time I represented a country in an international sports contest.

At the National Athletics Championships held in July 1968, the two outstanding track athletes were Martin Matupi of the Malawi Police, who ran the

100-metre sprint and Richard Nandolo of Malosa Secondary School, whose event was the 800 metres. Both dominated their events for years and eventually participated in Malawi's first international athletics Championships, the Commonwealth Games in Edinburgh in 1970. The only medal Malawi won at the Edinburgh Games was a bronze medal awarded to a member of the Malawi boxing team. Neither Matupi nor Nandolo, although recognized champions in Malawi, had sufficient training to match the qualities of the competitors they faced at the Edinburgh Games.

I continued through the rest of 1968 in the role of Southern Region sports organizer. In addition to organizing the regional and national sports events in athletics, basketball, cross country and netball, I travelled frequently on my faithful, and always unnamed motorcycle, to many secondary schools from Mlanje to Ncheu. On these trips, I was asked by Batchelor to assist in training and organizing competitions at secondary schools in sports such as athletics, basketball, cross-country and netball. I avoided football as this was politically charged then, as it is today. On my travels, I would usually stay at the houses of the Peace Corps teachers at the secondary schools I visited. This allowed me to eat well and share Greens (Carlsberg opened a new brewery in Malawi in the summer or1967. Its first offering had a green label; hence it became known as a Green) with my Peace Corps friends. This is the closest I got to teaching in the rural secondary schools where the rest of my Malawi X Peace Corps colleagues were living and having the times of their lives.

Reflections

Did I make the right choice moving from teaching in a classroom to teaching and organizing sports in an urban setting? Not only did I miss the unique and irreplaceable experience of a two-year stint in rural Malawi, I also spent the majority of my time in the biggest city in the country. When I questioned the relevance of my Peace Corps experience in the summer of 1967 while watching a schools sports competition in Blantyre with the new Director, Monroe McKay, he used his legal acumen and wisdom to convince me that my role in Blantyre was as important, nay more important, than I would have had elsewhere. I acquired many skills during my two years as a Peace Corps Volunteer which assisted me in meeting life's challenges. In future years, I used my sports knowledge from Malawi to participate in and organize sports in Kenya, Russia and other parts of the world. Most of all, I fell in love with Malawi and Malawians and a particular Malawian. Without Blantyre and my sports organization job, I wouldn't be writing these words in 2020.

Completed: October 20, 2020

AFRICAN GAME(S)

Snort. Snort. I froze. It was dark, a starless sky on a cloudy October night. Snort. Snort. Again. I couldn't move. Could barely breathe. Keep this thought. We'll return to it later in the memories of my adventures with African game.

Game parks, nature reserves, rain forests. All part of Africa's legacy to the world. Full of flora and fauna which are unknown elsewhere on our great and diverse planet. The biodiversity of Africa fortunately is captured in protected areas, despite the endless abuses and ravages by national governments, local governments, local populations, individual poachers; humanity more interested in personal profit than perpetual protection of species unique to the world.

Walking Safari in Luangwa

By the end of September, 1968, my two-year stint with the Peace Corps was almost over. One of my law school classmates, Mark, accompanied by his new bride, Irene, arranged with me to visit Malawi, Zambia and Rhodesia for three weeks in October. I would accompany them everywhere. The Ford Corsair we rented for this trip proved to be the bane of our existence. We had over 20 flat tires during the trip. No more mention of this burden need be made.

After ten days of touring Northern and Central Malawi, we crossed into Zambia at the border at Chipata and drove for two and a half hours to the Mfuwe Game Lodge in the Luangwa Game Reserve. At the time, Zambia had one of Africa's largest black rhino populations, with about one-third of a total population of 12,000 African rhinos living in the beautiful and wildlife-rich Luangwa Valley region. By 1998, thanks to rampant poaching and government indifference, rhinos were declared extinct in Zambia. Mine is a rhino story from 1968, when there were rampant rhino populations, not rampant poaching and destruction of the same.

We spent three days at Mfuwe, resting and enjoying the ambiance of hot and dry spring days before the rains. Equally soothing was the friendly and genuine hospitality of the staff of the Game Lodge. At that time, walking safaris were permitted in Zambia. We decided that rather than riding in our already puncture-tired car, we would have less stress and go on a walking safari. From the moment that we met our guard/guide, that choice was questionable; apprehension was rife.

At the front door of the Lodge, we readied ourselves for the jaunt we thought we were going to have. We were introduced to our walking guide, Samuel. He was in his forties, five feet one inches tall in heels and dressed to kill in a safari outfit which appeared to be from the 1950s film, Bhowani Junction. Khaki everything, baggy but somehow stiff shorts that hid his skinny, spindly legs, a tattered safari jacket, a safari hat of biblical proportions and his security for our walk -- a rifle. A rifle that might have last been fired during the Crimean War. A worn and scratched wooden stock, a tarnished and dull wrought iron barrel, and a leather strap that Samuel used to keep the rifle balanced on his thin and not very ample shoulder. Our initial thought was that Samuel was not the person to ensure our safety on this walking safari. But we were assured that he was experienced and knew how to use his rifle (if it would ever fire) in the event of an emergency. With less confidence than a Peace Corps Volunteer should have, I led Mark and Irene out into the bush, behind the intrepid Samuel.

Our first stop wasn't far up the road. We found a five foot tall termite hill, coloured the deep reddish, brownish orange of the local soil. Samuel explained to us the biology of termite hills, and their place in the ecology of a game park. At least he explained it according to his rural expertise in the 1960s. His view was that termites, in building their earthen towers, were using the natural daily temperature cycles to do the work of ventilating the mound for the termites – essentially creating a type of cooling engine that requires no energy input from the termites themselves. More modern research has determined that the primary function of the termite mound is to facilitate the exchange of carbon dioxide and oxygen, as opposed to regulating temperature. One of my lost or misplaced photographs is of Samuel, standing erect on the termite mound, rifle a'shouldered, and his hand over his eyes under his massive hat as he scanned the horizon, scouting the terrain ahead for animals and other dangers.

We were soon on the march. Samuel in the lead, followed by myself, and lastly Mark and Irene, inveterate New Yorkers, straggling behind and no doubt wondering why they decided to end their days in the Zambia bush. Through the scrub grass, past the ever-present acacia trees, walking along paths worn by animal meanderings over endless years, we wandered deeper and deeper into the Luangwa bush. It was mid-morning and already the burning sun made each stop in the shade of a tree a pleasurable respite. We were warned by Samuel to keep our chatter to a minimum, so that we wouldn't be heard by the game we sought as we trundled through the bush. Imagine telling New Yorkers to be quiet. Oh well.

As we were walking through the bush, Samuel stopped suddenly. Put his hand up to silence us. He froze but did not explain why. Slowly he gestured by nodding his head to a point in front of us. It took me a moment to understand why he was stiff and quiet. Not more than thirty yards ahead of us were two gray beings, one massive and one smaller than us. They were standing in the shade of a tree. Slowly I realized that we were within a short charge of a rhino mother and her baby. The baby was walking about, playful according to its age. But the mother stood as frozen as Samuel. Two beings who knew of each other even though the rhino's poor eyesight couldn't see him or us. The rhino mother's profile made it clear that she felt something not natural. Fortunately, Samuel's bush acumen worked better than his rifle (I'm sure); he had been walking with us into the wind. So we were diluting the mother's strong sense of smell by having our odours blown backwards with the wind.

It wasn't just the shaking of my knees and the scampering beat of my heart. Those were enough to make me freeze. I was truly in awe of the 4,000 pounds of living, motherly flesh. More pointedly, in awe of the horn which appeared to be like a stiletto, capable of piercing my essence and the essence of those with me.

I began sweating as I slowly took my camera out of its case. When confronted with a death wish, first thing I thought of – I need a photo of this. I checked the settings (this was a pre-iPhone world), all my movements like a Marcel Marceau performance. The wind was blowing softly into our faces, the heat of the bush was all around us, dust swirling from the dry, brown landscape. I eventually focused the camera, took a few, hurried photos and then put the camera quietly away. If I had to run, I didn't want to be fooling around with the camera. All four of us were fixed; we didn't move for an immeasurable time. Even the New Yorkers were quiet (it took a rhino mother to accomplish the impossible). We all watched the frolicking baby rhino, who was oblivious to the dangers that his mother felt.

After we had been entranced by the theatre of the African bush for uncountable minutes, the rhino mother and child moved away from us. Sweat was still pouring from me; and my heartbeat took more than a few minutes to return to its normal cadence. The rest of our walking safari was interrupted only by a few birds and smaller and safer-to-be-around game. It was the proverbial walk in the park. Yet this visit and the rhino incident is a montage which has remained locked in my memory for over fifty years.

Nairobi National Park

Ten years later, in 1978, it was time for my next rhino adventure in Africa. I had started working for First National City Bank of New York on July 1, 1975 after completing a three-and-a-half-year stint at the World Bank in Washington, DC. A year later, some clever, well-paid and no doubt soon wealthy brand maker came up with a new name for the bank: Citibank. From then on I was a Citibanker. After an intensive, three-month training program in New York City, I was posted to Nairobi, Kenya in October 1975 with my family, at that time my Malawian wife, Sherry, and our two very young daughters, Samantha and Melissa.

My boss in Nairobi was Bob Grant, a banker with Citibank for three decades who was then in charge of the bank's build out in Africa. The office I joined was called the African Regional Office (ARO). Bob and his wife, Marian, were experienced, overseas hands. He started his career in China in the late 1940s and was a logical choice for what was to become the Citibank expansion into Africa, managed by the team in ARO.

One of Bob's welcoming gestures for each new family was the required visit to Nairobi National Park. On a Sunday afternoon, he and Marian picked us up at our rented apartment in town and drove twenty-five minutes to the Park entrance on Langata Road. "Drove" is a calm word as we really sped on less than even but tarred roads to the entrance to the Park. My kids were freaking out as I never drove that fast. Somehow, we arrived safely, paid the entrance fees and entered the glorious ambiance of Nairobi National Park. Our adventure with Bob and Marian that afternoon was a welcome introduction to the game in the Park, and aside from the driving, a good way to bond with my future boss.

Nairobi National Park was established in 1946. It is just over four miles south of Nairobi. It is fenced on three sides, leaving the southern boundary open to allow migrating wildlife to move between the Park and the adjacent Kitengela plain, home to the Maasai people. Herbivores gather in the park during the dry season as there are some water holes strategically placed. This means that carnivores similarly gather at the same time as they have both water and meat on the menu.

Three years later I took the family, which now included 2-year-old Natasha, to Nairobi National Park for an afternoon of game viewing. In our white Peugeot 504 wagon, we travelled from our home at the Boit House in Kileleshwa to the entrance to the Park. At a normal speed. It was a weekend afternoon and all were in good spirits.

Our usual gambit was to enter the park, head to the left and do a broad sweep on the outside road around the Park. From time to time, we spotted various game, stopped, viewed, photographed, chatted and enjoyed an afternoon few in the world get to experience. On this afternoon, our enjoyment was tested.

On each visit, before driving around, we would stop at the orphanage inside the Park near the gate. Many animals that had been rescued by the Park rangers were kept in the orphanage until they could be rehabilitated or recover from injuries they might have incurred. One of our favourite animals to visit was the rhino, whose name escapes me but who had been in the orphanage for many years. He would stand near the fence where we stopped and allow us to touch his hide. I would say "pet", but that's not a word I would use with a rhino. The hide was as hard as rock; we would tap it with our hands and fists. The rhino was impervious to our touching adventure. He would stoically remain in position, as we each had our go at his hide. We learned early on that a rhino hide is no different than a piece of granite.

Our rhino meetings in the orphanage were on our minds as we stopped that day on a dirt road. I was driving, as usual. When I stopped the car, I kept the engine running.

Somewhere in my head I remembered that one should never stop a car in a game park and turn off the engine. I was looking at a map of the Park when the kids, from the back seat, shouted about something behind us. I looked in the rear-view mirror and saw, on the same dirt road about forty yards away, two gray beings. Two rhinos. A mother and a child. Déjà vu. Just like in Luangwa a decade before.

The girls were getting scared, and made enough noise to convince me of this. What did I do? Well, again I wanted a photo of the rhinos, which were not easy to see in the open veldt of Nairobi National Park. It was very unusual to see them standing on the road. While my daughters were making enough noise to bother the rhino mother, I fumbled with my camera and a 200mm telephoto lens so that I could lean out the window and snap photos of the rhinos. I was just about done getting the equipment ready when the mother rhino decided to charge our car. As she started toward the car, I leaned out of the window, looked backward at a ludicrous angle and attempted as best I could to focus on the rhinos and take some photos. As I clicked the camera for the last time, with my daughters and wife screaming in my ears, I hit the accelerator and moved away with a rush. The rhino mother was about ten feet from the car when I started moving forward. My family cursed me for risking all of our lives for a photo. Maybe my car felt the same.

I don't know what bothered me more, my pounding heart, my sweaty palms or the endless barrage of complaints from the ladies in the car. I was called many things that I won't repeat here. We had barely escaped the horn of a dilemma, which was created solely by me and my arrogance as a wildlife photographer.

Ngorongoro Fright

It was a trip of celebration, specifically Hal's 60th birthday. Son Niles wanted to share Africa with him. I had become a business friend and then a personal friend of Niles after our first meeting in 1976 when I was living in Nairobi with my young family. It was now 1978 and Niles proposed to visit Tanzania with his faither to celebrate dad's birthday.

From my Nairobi base, I had been making frequent trips to Tanzania. Niles got in touch with me and asked if I would be in Tanzania at the beginning of October 1978 and if so, he invited me to join him and Hal on a week's holiday in Tanzania. It was an easy decision.

Well, the decision was easy but the ability to get from Nairobi to Dar-es-Salaam was not. In July 1977, the three States comprising the East African Community (EAC), an early but eventually unsuccessful attempt at African unity, decided to go their separate ways. Kenya wanted more power in the decision-making organs of the EAC because of its strong economy. This led to disagreements between the three member States. The real reasons for the collapse were the different economic systems, primarily between capitalist Kenya, socialist Tanzania and autocratic and non-conforming Uganda.

Their disagreements arose also from the unique personalities of President Jomo Kenyatta of Kenya, President Julius Nyerere of Tanzania and the craziness and inconsistency of President Idi Amin Dada of Uganda.

How did the collapse of the EAC manifest itself? Here's one example. In late July 1977, I was at Nairobi Airport, ready to board a flight to Zambia. I was working with Citibank in Nairobi at that time and two of my biggest customers were the two mining giants of Zambia, NCCM and RCM. I was in Zambia almost every month, meeting with senior executives and looking for further lending opportunities. Waiting for the East African Airlines (EAA) flight that morning, I started talking to the Sudanese Ambassador to Kenya, Francis Deng, who was on the same flight. When the flight was called and we started to leave the departure lounge, an EAA representative approached all the passengers. His message was simple. The budget of the EAC was not approved, so if we wanted to fly that day to Lusaka, each passenger would have to pay, on the spot, Sh.600 ($75) to cover fuel costs. Both Ambassador Deng and I refused, retrieved our luggage and headed back to the Nairobi city centre. The EAC was kaput and EAA died along with it.

The mists of time have obscured the route I took to get to Dar-es-Salaam from Nairobi so that I could meet Hal and Niles at the start of our safari. The border had been closed since July 1977, and airlines had to find unique routes in order to carry their passengers from Nairobi to neighbouring countries. Neither Kenya nor Tanzania permitted their respective new airlines, Kenya Airways and Air Tanzania, to use the air space of the other country. Hal and Niles flew into Dar from London on British Airways. I must have found some clever way to get there, as I was in Dar-es-Salaam when they landed.

In Dar-es-Salaam, the three of us stayed at the Motel AGIP, a three-star facility right in the centre of town. The Motel AGIP was owned and managed by Noli Mantheakis, my close Tanzanian-born friend. Noli and I first met in March 1978 and have remained close friends until today. The restaurant at the Motel AGIP was the best in Dar. It was called the restaurant; no other name. The rooms of the Motel AGIP were spartan. The day before we left on our safari, we had a celebration lunch at the restaurant. The crab at this restaurant was always the best dish in Dar, and Noli made sure our palates were tested as we tasted the varieties of ways one can prepare crab.

At that time, Niles was founder and President of Equator Bank, based in Hartford, Connecticut, USA. Equator Bank had a few clients in Tanzania. One of them was Rajpar, who owned a car dealership in Dar. Rajpar decided to add to the birthday celebration by sending a case of wine to the restaurant while we were eating lunch. Hal was thrilled that someone would bother to give him a case of wine for any reason. Niles and I were a bit more sceptical. When we opened the case, we found twelve bottles of the latest vintages of Dodoma Rose and Dodoma Red, two local brands that were touted in Tanzania as their threat to the French dominance of the wine industry. We opened one bottle of Dodoma Rose to drink with our meal. One sip, and Hal decided to donate the remaining eleven and two-thirds bottles to wine heaven. One sip, that's all it took. It brought back to Niles and me memories of the first Ethiopian wine crop that we had tasted. North of South Africa, the wine industry was an infant.

We flew to Arusha in a small plane as we began our safari. We got into a Land Rover and had a long ride to a lodge in Mikumi National Park. Riding through the bush on dirt roads on a hot afternoon, bouncing over every ridge, swerving to avoid potholes, we arrived at the lodge at six o'clock that evening, rather exhausted. As we unbundled from our Land Rover in front of the main building of the lodge, a young, thin and smiling man came out to greet us. With confidence well beyond his years, he held his hand up as we stood before him and announced: "Number 1, welcome. Number 2, the Rules!" Whereupon he went into a five-minute lecture about what we could do and not do, when we could do or not do it and where we could do or not do it. His welcome has been become one of my favourite greetings for years.

After a nice visit to Mikumi National Park, our next stop was at Lake Manyara National Park. This park is known for its tree climbing lions. Lions climb trees in most game parks in Africa, but Lake Manyara has made their presence above the ground part of the mantra they recite to all visitors. Most lions are not good tree climbers and find that coming down is not as easy as going up. Sounds like most people who climb things. We stayed at the Lake Manyara Kilimamoja Lodge. In fact, we were the only three guests. At that time, Tanzania was going through both economic and political turmoil and tourism had fallen to historically low levels. The staff at the hotel gave us the royal treatment, which befitted our safari in honour of Hal's birthday.

We then drove to Ngorongoro Crater Lodge, which is located on a ridge overlooking the spectacular Ngorongoro Crater, which is the largest inactive, intact and unfilled volcanic caldera in the world. The crater is two thousand feet deep, and consists of an area of one hundred square miles. The Ngorongoro Conservation Area is a UNESCO World Heritage Site. In 1892 Oscar Baumann was the first European to visit Ngorongoro Crater. After World War I, two German brothers, Adolph and Friedrich Siedentopf, established a farm on six thousand hectares within the Crater. The first time the Crater was made a conservation area was in 1948.

Our stay at the lodge was fabulous, except for one event. Niles got deathly ill, some form of food poisoning which did not affect Hal or myself. The next morning, while Hal and I toured the crater in a Land Rover, Niles only had strength to view the crater from his room on the lip of the Crater. Niles and Hal had rooms in the main building, while I was staying in a nearby one-story building comprised of a series of rooms, motel-like in design. Mine was in the middle, about fifty yards from the first room.

We had dinner, although Niles looked pekid and hardly ate anything. Hal and I recounted the wonderful day on the floor of the Crater. We toasted each other with non-Dodoma wine and tales of the zebra, wildebeest, various deer, buffalo, lions and endless birds that had filled our memories. We were excited to tell Niles all that he had missed. At about ten o'clock that evening, I was tired and excused myself from our after dinner gathering. I was tired after a long day and needed some sleep. Little did I know what lay ahead.

I walked out of the main building. There were few lights and I could barely find the long building in which my room was located. I got to the edge of the building when I heard: Snort. Snort. I froze. It was dark, a starless sky on a cloudy October night. Snort. Snort. Again. I couldn't move; could barely breathe. I had no idea what animal was waiting for me. Nor was I anxious to find out.

Frozen to the spot, I waited for my eyes to adjust to the darkness. Every second seemed endless. I heard a swishing noise like an animal moving in the grass. Then again. Snort. Snort. My heart was beating fast, and my eyes still hadn't found my nemesis. I took a step. Then waited. I took another step. Waited again. Time seemed to extend itself. I was only conscious of the noise of an animal which I still couldn't find.

After I had taken about five small steps, and much time had passed, I finally found the snorting source. It was a large cape buffalo, one of the most dangerous animals in Africa, standing on a small incline, about twenty feet left from me. In the depth of night, with the effects of the dinner wine still in me, I was truly afraid. Embarrassingly afraid. Heart pumping, eyes trying to focus, I tried to calculate how long it would take me to get to my room. I had passed the first two rooms of the building, but had three more to pass before getting to my room. At the speed I thought I was going, it seemed it would take all night.

Nervously taking a step every minute or two, and feeling the buffalo getting closer with every step, I had no confidence that I could get into the room before being attacked by the buffalo. All manner of scenarios sped through my head. None ended well. I was sweating profusely as well as nervous and fearful.

Eventually, I moved closer to my room. The key was in my pocket, a small, metal key attached to a large, wooden block which served as a keyholder. It was awkward, heavy and had my room number etched into the wood. It was in my pocket, stuck there because of its size. Now I had to find a way to get the key out of my pocket without disturbing my buffalo friend. I was at the door, fumbling with the key and trying to watch the buffalo at the same time. I tried to put the key in the lock, but I had it upside down. More seconds wasted as I stood at the door. Terror-filled thoughts going through my head. I finally got the key into the lock, and slowly turned it. It made a noise, but the door opened.

As I opened the door and stepped into the room, I forgot that there were immediately at the door two steps down to the floor. I was so anxious to get into the room that I missed the steps and fell clumsily down to the floor below. I was so nervous that I didn't feel the scrapes on my knees and elbow. I also didn't notice in the dark that the floor, which was made of cement, had been waxed smooth with a green, boot polish. As I slid down and along the floor, my hands and clothes rubbed in the green polish and made sure I would never forget that entry into the room. My glasses also fell off, landing near me on the polished green cement. I recovered quickly to reach up and close the door. My buffalo friend could have joined me at any time, as I had forgotten to close the door as I slid into the room. Recovery took a long time. Deep breaths, and many prayers later, my heartbeat had finally come down to normal. My sleep that night was punctured with dreams of what might have happened if I hadn't gotten into the room before the buffalo. My green polished clothes stood testimony to what did happen.

While we were at Ngorongoro Crater Lodge, another event affected our trip. Tanzania and Uganda declared war against each other on October 9. All of a sudden, I had no way to get home. Niles and his dad were going to fly from Arusha to Dar-es-Salaam and then fly up to London. I called my friend Noli and asked him how I could get back to Kenya. Noli had obtained his pilot's license a few years before and spent many hours each month in a small plane over the African bush. When I called back to ask what he recommended, he said that he would fly up to Arusha, pick me up in his plane and fly me to Mombasa, on the Kenyan coast. Small planes were permitted to enter each country's air space. I would then catch an internal Kenya Airways flight back to Nairobi. It was either go with Noli or be stuck in Tanzania. I gratefully accepted Noli's offer.

Noli arrived at Arusha Airport the next day, late morning. He came inside and we had a coffee together with Niles and Hal, before their flight to Dar-es-Salaam. Then we walked out to the apron, got into his two-seater airplane, attached our seat belts and headed into the wild blue yonder. The flight took about 90 minutes. At one point Noli gave me the stick and said, "fly the plane". Of course he kept his feet on the rudder pedals. After two minutes, and shaking like a guy who just saw a buffalo outside his door, I handed the stick back to Noli. What a relief! The end to my Tanzanian holiday was rather pedestrian. After Noli dumped me at Mombasa Airport, I bought a ticket on the next flight to Nairobi and was home for dinner that night. Secure in a house without green polish on the floor and able to sleep without hearing Snort Snort in the dark! A perfect end to another African game adventure.

Four Minutes from Maasai Mara

It was Saturday, February 16, 1980. As it happened, a total solar eclipse occurred that day–for us without warning. A solar eclipse occurs when the moon passes between earth and the sun, thereby totally or partially obscuring the image of the sun for a viewer on earth. A total solar eclipse occurs when the moon's apparent diameter is larger than the sun's diameter, blocking all direct sunlight and turning day into darkness.

My older brother, Bob, had come to Kenya to visit us. To celebrate his first and only visit to Kenya, we decided to go game viewing in the Maasai Mara National Reserve, considered by many to be the best game reserve in Kenya. One reason for this opinion is that Maasai Mara sits on the northern border of Serengeti National Park in Tanzania, which is a vast nature reserve known not only for its annual wildebeest and zebra migrations, but also for its lions, elephants and rhinos. Maasai Mara is a similar area of preserved savannah wilderness. The game populating its borders include lions, cheetahs, elephants, small and large deer, zebras and hippos. Wildebeest traverse its plains during their annual migration. The landscape has grassy plains and rolling hills, and is crossed by the Mara and Talek Rivers. The area nearby is dotted with villages of Maasai people.

We had just spent four days visiting Maasai Mara and its incredible game. We stayed at Governor's Camp, well known at that time for bringing visitors close to nature, without the extravagant luxuries provided by some of the other camps in the Mara.

After an early breakfast, we packed our bags and the kids into the car, and left Governor's Camp around 9:30 am in the morning. It was a sunny day, and we were filled with the memories and delights of eyeing African game for the past several days. We also enjoyed the food and camaraderie which is present in every game park camp. The trip to our Kileleshwa home in Nairobi would take a minimum of six hours. As we maneuvered along the road, we chatted; the kids naturally were rambunctious. Normality on a family outing, whether in the US, Europe or Africa. The car windows were open as we enjoyed the breeze and the views of the savannah landscape.

Then all changed. Dramatically. Hard to describe how the sunlight started to fade. All was bright and beautiful. As the time neared 11:30 am, there was an unexpected loss of definition as we looked ahead. Even these words are not accurate. The world around us became emptier. Light was softer, almost translucent. This wasn't the only sense of foreboding. The noises of the bush, which we could hear even as the wind rushed through the car windows, suddenly went quiet. Fading light, and disappearing noise.

We stopped the car on the side of the road. As we got out and looked up in the sky, we could see the edge of the moon already moving across the face of the sun. It was like a dark poker chip flying above. Little by little, the area of the sun covered by the moon increased. As this happened, the light became ephemeral, even eerie, as if we were closer to night than noon. All noise from the bush stopped. The six of us outside the car stood in awe of nature's latest theatrical presentation; the darkening of the day as the moon covered more and more of the sun.

Since we had no foreknowledge of the solar eclipse, we were surprised when it occurred. Standing on a quiet African road in the middle of Kenya, with the open veldt all around us, we could hear nothing except our own voices. All birds decided that it was night time and they ceased their songs and calls. All insects ended their chirpings and buzzings. None of the animals were inclined to roar or bark or wail. 11:30 am and all went into night mode. It was surreal.

Within a few minutes, the entire landscape was dark. And quiet. Above, the moon now covered the sun, a full solar eclipse. No eye protection was necessary; no darkened glass needed to cover our eyes. We were smack dab in the centre of the 100 mile wide path of the eclipse. For a period of just over four minutes, we stood silently, all of us bound by nature's artistry. Instead of the sun, we saw the moon, surrounded by a bright, yellow orange ring of sunlight. A ring of fire. A golden glow around a black circle. Dark and light. Light and dark. And all the while, not a sound to be heard except our breathing and the occasional voices of the kids in our own bubble. A magical moment to be remembered forever.

Slowly the moon moved further to the left as we watched. Little by little, the sun awoke again, ready to fulfil its promise to throw light on planet earth as if the start of a new day. The black patch of the moon became smaller and smaller. The heat of the sun touched our faces as its brilliance returned to re-ignite the Kenyan landscape. In an inkling, birds and insects woke from their short slumbers and saturated the air with their songs, callings, chirpings and buzzings. Life which had shut down completely for four minutes awoke again with a vengeance. The African theatre was back in session.

Completed October 20, 2020

AROUND (MOST OF) THE WORLD IN 80 DAYS

"A journey of a thousand miles begins with a single step". Not a quote from Confucius, as I thought, but from his 6th century B.C. contemporary, Lao Tsu. Every trip has a beginning, middle and end, yet every trip is different. Even though each trip begins with that first single step.

My round-the-world adventure began curiously in 1963, when I first decided I wanted to join the U.S. Peace Corps. My father was outspokenly against my forsaking the chance of a legal education at Harvard Law School for a two-year stint in the Peace Corps. So we agreed that after my Harvard legal education, he would support whatever life choices I made. For this reason, I deferred my Peace Corps application until the last semester of law school which began in January 1966. I never regretted this delay as I ended up with five amazing gifts: a Harvard legal education, my Peace Corps years in Malawi, a wife, four lovely daughters and one halfway round the world trip. Thanks Dad.

Throughout Peace Corps training in Syracuse, New York in the Fall of 1966, and during the first year of my new life in Malawi, beginning January 1, 1967, the furthest thing from my mind was how to get back to the U.S. after my contract with the Peace Corps ended -- and what to do when I returned. I enjoyed my Peace Corps life so much that it never occurred to me that it would end. Each day was more fascinating, more unique, more unusual than the previous day. Each day I made new friends. Each day I learned new things. Each day I was privileged not only to see the growth of a new nation, but to participate in making that growth meaningful -- for me, for my Malawi X Peace Corps colleagues, and for the many people I met in Malawi. This is the wonder, the joy and the strength of the Peace Corps.

In January 1968, during school holidays after my first year of teaching, I met my law school roommate, Eddie, in Mombasa, Kenya and Dar-es-Salaam, Tanzania. We then started communicating about what we would do after our Peace Corps days were over. He and his wife, Ellie, were teaching in Liberia. Since we were on the same continent, one option was to meet somewhere and make more history together. We really enjoyed our East African experiences that January.

During 1968, Eddie and I wrote to each other by letter; we also exchanged audio tapes. All of the possible apres-Peace Corps options, including an African safari, a European adventure or a luxury liner from the UK to the US, soon fell away. I met Sherry in May 1968, at a Lions Club May Fayre. We started dating in July 1968. Within sixteen months, Sherry and I would marry. I accepted a job offer in November 1968 to serve as Treaties Officer in Malawi's Ministry of External Affairs. One reason for this was I wanted to spend more time with Sherry. I was now on the hook for at least thirty more months in a country I loved and was therefore unable to take advantage of any of the travel options which had been under consideration for most of 1968.

As I got closer to the June 1971 termination date in my contract with the Malawi Government, Sherry and I started to consider options that were not available earlier. In accordance with the contract I had signed, I was to be paid by the Malawi Government a gratuity in lieu of a pension. Based upon my salary of $6,000 per year, this meant I would receive from the Malawi Government a lump sum of $5,000 in addition to the air tickets home for Sherry and myself. What to do with $5,000? Go straight back to the US, settle somewhere, buy a car, and begin a business and home life in some city in the US? Or, be more adventurous, take the $5,000, and purchase the extra cost of returning to the US going East from Malawi by airplane until we got to the West Coast of the US?

We eventually decided (probably I decided and Sherry did not object too much, although she had neither been outside Malawi nor on an airplane) to take a long trip through the following countries before arriving in the US: Mauritius, Kenya, Israel, Iran, Afghanistan, India (and Kashmir), Thailand, Taiwan, Japan, and the following cities after arriving in the US: Honolulu, Los Angeles, San Francisco, Phoenix, Chicago, New York and Washington, D.C. Nine countries and seven cities in the US. And by the way, Sherry found out she was pregnant in April 1971, two months before our planned departure. Perfect timing!

Unbundling from one's place of residence is not an easy task. We took what we could carry with us for the long trip home, which was minimal. The rest of our earthly possessions, which again were not many, we shipped back to my parents' home outside of Chicago to await our arrival there in early Fall. Sherry got extremely nervous about leaving her home for the first time; she started to have second thoughts and complained many times to her mother and other family members. But this was not as bad as when she agreed to marry me. At that time, her nervousness led to her having shingles three weeks before our wedding. A painful reminder of pre-marital bliss.

Being pregnant also made planning for the trip complicated, and dangerous. Sherry would often make strange requests (strange to me, not her) about almost everything. This became exacerbated during the trip, as the pressures of travel and pregnancy took their toll. It didn't help that this was my first "pregnancy" as well; I wasn't prepared for the unusual requests about such things as food, sleep, heat, cold, smells, noise and clothes. I don't think I did any better with daughters number two to four in later years, but at least we were not on an around the world trip during later pregnancies.

Chileka Airport was not a large place in 1971. The new airport in Lilongwe was not even an imagination. The terminal at Chileka was cosy and crowded that June afternoon, cooler because it was the middle of winter. I remember seeing all of Sherry's family at the airport. A virtual who's who of the Hassen family (and endless other close and not so close relatives). She was full of tears and fears in the terminal (while her family was full of beers) but once we had settled into our seats (I gave her the window seat for her first flying adventure), Sherry became more relaxed. Well, as relaxed as any pregnant woman could be on her first trip in an airplane. We were on our way to Mauritius, the Lao Tsu single step.

Mauritius

I was quite fortunate that my work for the Ministry of External Affairs over the previous thirty months had brought me into contact with Regis, the Director of Tourism in Mauritius. I met Regis first in 1970 and we formed a close personal bond. It was Regis who suggested that we visit Mauritius on the first leg of our return to the US. We went from a small puddle at Chileka Airport in Malawi to an even smaller puddle at the air terminal on Mauritius. When we saw Regis' smiling face in the crowd upon landing, both of us felt like we had come home. In fact, to some extent we had. We were taken to Rose Hill where Regis and Margaret, his English wife, lived. They insisted that Sherry and I have their bedroom, while they slept in the living room on a sofa. For a whole week we were in our home, our bed, our family. Regis and Margaret saw to that. What a wonderful way to cushion the shock of Sherry's first international trip.

Mauritius is a paradise for tourists and here we were, living with the Director of Tourism, who was hell bent on ensuring that we saw all one could see on this fabulous island playground. During our one week stay, we saw about a dozen amazing hotels, endless restaurants (while still enjoying Margaret's home cooking many evenings), the Port Louis racecourse, the Pamplemousses botanical gardens, and the colourful, noisy, teeming food market in Rose Hill. There seemed to be no end to the wonders of Mauritius, all delivered to us by a personal tour with the main tourism expert in the country.

One day we visited a hotel on the east side of the island. We needed to get into a flat-bottomed boat to get from the car park to the hotel. A one-hundred-yard boat ride to heaven on earth. The five-star hotel was built on a small island, a haven of peace on an already peaceful island. For lunch, Regis and I tore into a plate of raw clams that seemed feet high. Sherry could not fathom why raw clams would be a food and stuck to something meatier. Or maybe it was her belly yelling for such morsels. We finished the entire clam-high plate, showing that I had learned nothing from my earlier encounter in Malawi with Portuguese boxing promoters with appetites for mountains of piri piri prawns.

Regis and I had our comeuppance a day or so later. We went to the west of the island and had fried scallops for lunch. Sherry once again refused to indulge. This time her instinct was correct. By late night, Regis and I were deathly ill, vomiting and doing other nasty things, feeling miserable for ourselves. Sherry gloated. In the morning after a sleepless night, Regis said he had the perfect cure for our bad tummies. He cooked us a soup with herbs and other things from a recipe his mother had given him years before. Its smell was enticing, even to people as sick as Regis and I were. Miraculously, one hour after sipping this miracle soup, Regis and I were fit again, and ready for the next adventure on his island home.

As one would imagine, a seven-day visit on an island paradise accompanied by the Director of Tourism was like winning the lottery. At every location we were treated as special guests. All doors opened quickly. What most amazed me was the informality of Mauritius and the close relationship between Regis and everyone we met. He seemed to know every person on the island by name. This was brought to a head on our last day on the island, a Sunday. We left early for Pamplemousses Botanical Garden, now called Sir Seewoosagur Ramgoolam Botanical Garden, which is located near the capital, Port Louis. The most amazing features of this garden were the giant lily pads, which were said to be strong enough to hold an eight pound baby. We hadn't had any babies yet, so we couldn't test the theory. That would have been a good test for Samantha, then residing in her mother's womb, as she was four ounces under eight pounds when born, although I cannot fathom why anyone would place a baby on a lily pad, no matter what its alleged weight-bearing properties were.

We finished our tour around eleven in the morning. Regis was driving us in his own car; we had no other plans until our flight at four in the afternoon. He asked if we wanted to have tea with the Prime Minister, the already famous Sir Seewoosagur Ramgoolam, even though the unbuilt new airport hadn't yet been named after him. I looked at Sherry and said, let's do it. Regis stopped the car on the road, went to a telephone box, put in a coin and called the Prime Minister. Regis said he was with some important international visitors and asked if the Prime Minister would have time to see us. Sundays must have been slow in those days as we were invited immediately to go to State House for a cuppa. Thirty minutes later, we were in the gracious presence of the Prime Minister, chatting away about Mauritius and other things. When the tea service was brought out, the Prime Minister asked Sherry to pour cups of tea for each of us, as that is a woman's job. She did so with a smile on her face. We were there for two hours, in the ambience of State House, the presence of the most senior politician on this tropical island country, sipping tea while munching biscuits with Sir Seewoosagur Ramgoolam himself. He must have made one heck of an impact on the country as today the new airport, the Botanical Garden and many other things are named after this gentle, kind and tea-loving, but not tea-pouring, man.

After our State House tea party, we went back to Rose Hill, picked up our katundu (baggage) and headed to the airport. We were scheduled to fly on a Lufthansa flight to Nairobi, our next stop. The airport seemed quiet that afternoon. This was confirmed when we got on the aircraft and discovered that we were two of the four passengers flying on a B707 for the next four hours. We were outnumbered by the stewards and stewardesses. They proposed to open the champagne and other drinks for our liquid flight to Kenya. One of the happiest flights I have ever taken. Almost twenty attendants looking after four people on a plane that could seat almost two hundred. A few bottles of champagne met their deserved end.

Nairobi

We landed at Embakasi Airport, serving Nairobi, the capital of Kenya. On this leg of our long trip home, we stayed for a week with Bertha, one of Sherry's closest friends from Malawi who was living with Tommy, her Swedish husband. Tommy was employed by L.M. Ericsson, the Swedish telecoms company where he worked until his retirement decades later. The four of us had taken a trip to Zambia in January 1970, to see the Kariba Dam, Lake Kariba and the glory of Victoria Falls at Livingstone. This was long before the birth of their two sons and our four daughters.

In the hills of Zambia about ten miles north of Kariba Dam, we stopped on a dirt road to have our first full view of the Dam. Tommy got out of the front seat on his side of the car. As I got out from the driver's seat, I forgot to put the hand brake on. I was looking at the Dam when I realized that the car was starting to roll backwards, gravity showing its force because of the upward angle I had stopped on. I panicked and started running alongside the car as it picked up speed downhill. Sherry and Bertha were screaming from the seats in the back of the car. Somehow, I got the driver's door opened, jumped in and put my foot on the brake. Had I been a bit slower, the car certainly would have crashed into the hills below. The four of us were bound together in a special way after that experience.

Tommy and Bertha lived in a comfortable three bedroomed house in a Nairobi suburb, on a large plot off Argwings Kodhek Road. We slept long that first night before starting our Kenyan adventure. Little did we know that four years later, on an October day, we would arrive in Nairobi again, this time with two young daughters, for an eight year stay in the country. Tommy became our taxi driver, ferrying us around the capital as we partook of the many tourist attractions in this famous, tourist friendly city. This meant going to see the Nairobi National Park, just outside the city, the Bomas of Kenya dancing and cultural centre, the Kenyatta International Convention Centre, several restaurants, seeing many friends (including some of Tommy's colleagues at L.M. Ericsson, especially Antal who was a naturalized Swedish citizen from Hungary who left Hungary in 1956 during the infamous revolution against the Soviet invasion).

The week in Kenya sped by, as we were in the comfort of a private home with close friends from Malawi. We didn't feel like we were traveling. Sherry and Bertha had much to gossip about, as young ladies often do. Tommy and I discussed the world over a Tusker beer or two. Or three. The helter skelter days of our Mauritius adventure were replaced by the cosiness of our long friendship and a daily pace more attuned to living in a country, not visiting it. Soon however, the days stretched into the date of departure. We were leaving Africa and heading to other parts of the world. For Sherry this was an eye opener. The world, not Africa.

Tel Aviv

We were on an El Al flight. Every seat taken, mostly Israelis returning home from their business, technical assistance and humanitarian assistance assignments in Kenya. Possibly some tourists as well. The aircraft did not touch down at Lod Airport; it slammed down. The hardest landing I ever had in my life. Surprisingly the tires survived – at least that landing. Lod Airport had not yet changed its name to Ben Gurion International Airport; that would happen in 1973. As with most airports at the time, it was small, intimate, yet in Israel already with more security than one would see in any African airport.

We stayed with Gideon and his family. Gideon was a friend of my brother, Rick. They offered to host us while we were in Israel. This was fortunate, as it allowed us to live with a family and learn about life in Israel at that time. It was late June, approaching July, and the heat was intense. This was quite a change from Kenya, which was in the middle of its winter months in June. It was much colder in the highlands of Kenya than the coastal areas of Israel.

Because of the high-quality diamond industry in Israel, I wanted to buy Sherry a better engagement ring than the one Aaron helped get for us from Rhodesia. Aaron was an American lawyer from New York teaching students at the new Law School outside of Blantyre. Gideon's mother knew exactly where to go. She accompanied us to the dealer, helped us pick a ring which Sherry liked, and even more so, to obtain a discount so that the purchase would not swallow our meagre bank balance.

We stayed in Tel Aviv with Gideon's family. One day we took a tour on a bus with other visitors. I had an 8mm movie camera and took movies as our bus bounced along on the roads. Some of my worst films/photos ever came from that trip. Part of this tour required me to sit tefillin. The orthodox young man who helped me was surprised that a Jewish man like myself did not know how to put on the tefillin and pray. With his help, my prayers hopefully reached the place prayers go to.

We also went to Jerusalem for a day with Gideon and family. We went to all the required sites, for all three religions, prayed at the Wailing Wall, and had an amazing lunch, not only with great food but with musical entertainment which still rings in my ears. A warm, convivial day which made us feel like we were with family.

Tehran

Soon, our tour of Israel reached its departure date. Sadly, we left Gideon and family and headed for Tehran. Yes, Tehran! This would be surprising in today's hostile political climate but back then, Israel and Iran had friendly relations. Iran was the second country in the region to recognize Israel as a country after Turkey. We flew directly from Tel Aviv to Tehran. On El Al.

After the coup in the early 1950s, Iran was controlled by the Pahlavi dynasty. The famous leader of the country was the Shah of Iran, Mohammed Reza Shah, a pro-Western leader. When we arrived in Tehran, the most noticeable thing was the heat, the intense, very intense, but dry heat. It averaged over one hundred degrees Fahrenheit during our five-day stay in Tehran. Sherry was only three months pregnant but was overwhelmed by the heat. We spent a lot of our time in the air-conditioned hotel, as she tired quickly in the burning and relentless sun. For this reason, we limited our tours of the city. However, one tour has never left my memory.

On our third day in Tehran, even with the overpowering heat, we visited the Central Bank of Iran in which the Treasury of National Jewels is located. It is hard to describe what we found on three floors of this building. It is truly a treasure as much a treasury. Marvellous to behold and almost unbelievable. A collection of elaborate crowns, tiaras, plumes, bejewelled swords and shields, a seemingly endless number of unset precious gems, including diamonds and rubies and emeralds, numerous plates and other dining services cast in precious metals and encrusted with gems, and many unusual items such as the massive golden globe with the oceans made of emeralds. All had been collected or taken by Persian monarchs from the sixteenth century on. The uncut gemstones were piled on plates, often with gemstones over a foot high; seemingly thousands on each plate. Hundreds of such plates. Uncountable wealth.

The display of gems was overwhelming. For example, the Darya-e Noor, the Sea of Light diamond, 182 carats. The largest pink diamond in the world with a most unusual colour. This diamond had been kept in the Russian Embassy in Teheran for protection during one period of disturbances. Fortunately, this unique diamond was returned to the Government of Iran and remains one of the highlights of the Treasury. In 1971, the level of security for the endless waves of gemstones and the other contents of the Treasury was minimal. Mostly a number of security people posted all over the three floors as electronic security would have been non-existent at that time.

Other than the excitement of the Treasury, during our visit to Tehran we were mainly constrained by the heat and Sherry's pregnancy. Each feeding on the other. We were told of the Azadi Tower, a celebration of two thousand five hundred years of the foundation of the Persian Empire. But it was still under construction in July 1971 and was not opened to the public until the following year.

Kabul

The next leg of our journey was probably more my choice, because of the mystery of Afghanistan. Back in 1971, the connotations which arise today were not in the air. It was a mystical, magical, mountain kingdom in the middle of an area of the world that neither of us had thought or heard about. Afghanistan. Its lure rolled off our lips. Afghanistan. The flight from Tehran to Kabul was only two and a half hours, but it took us to an unknown time and place. The small and dilapidated airport gave no indication of the stark and barren country which would open itself to our eyes over the next couple days.

We asked the taxi driver to recommend a hotel. The first one we checked into was our hotel for an hour. That is the amount of time it took Sherry to see that the sheets on the bed were the same ones that the previous occupants had used. We checked out of that hotel so fast that our bags never made it to the room. Quickly we found a cleaner hotel. Quite in line with our budget (and my Peace Corps mindset) too. Two dollars a night; for a double. Breakfast included. Almost as cheap as our hotel in Dar-es-Salaam during my 1967 trip to Mount Kilimanjaro with my Peace Corps mates.

Kabul was as hot and dry as Tehran was during the previous week. It was just more mountainous. We decided to become tourists and hired a taxi to take us around the city. That's how we met Muneeb. For what seemed a pittance, Muneeb agreed to drive us around Kabul for three hours, including the city centre, gardens, and various viewpoints in the mountains. Fortunately his English was better than our Pashto, which allowed us to get the flavour of Kabul and its environs. He showed us all the places that tourists are wont to go. Because we were getting along so well (and no doubt the prospect of any other tourists was slim), he offered to take us to his home so that we could rest in the shade and have something to drink.

When we got to his home up in the hills, we had a wonderful view of the city and the valleys surrounding central Kabul. His home was in a large, open area cooled by many trees. I was told to lie down under the olive trees on large, colourful pillows which had been tossed asunder without rhyme or reason. Sherry was invited by Muneeb's wife into their house. I was not allowed to enter the house; only women were allowed inside. I fell into the embrace of a mammoth pillow, out of the burning sun and in the shade, and given my first drink of dugh. Yogurt like, but full of herbs and other things. It was tasty and refreshing. In addition, Muneeb served me sour cherries, a specialty in Afghanistan. He also gave me a drink called Sharbat-E-Olu Bolu, which was made from sour cherries. I was truly in heaven, lying in luxury, drinking local drinks, listening to fables of ancient history, lost in reveries as a mild breeze brushed my face. The climate did not seem oppressive anymore. Lying on a pillow, talking to Muneeb about life, family and Afghanistan. A pause within the pause of our long trip home. Who could ever imagine what the word Kabul would mean in August 2021.

On our next day in Kabul, we visited the Shahr-e Naw Park. An area of trees with a small stream flowing through the park. There were some children playing where we walked. We were fascinated by two young girls who were each blue-eyed, black haired and dark skinned. Strikingly beautiful. Like the Roth paintings in my parents' apartment in Florida years later. I guess we were shocked by the blue eyes, which stared at us as much as we stared at them.

We crashed most of that afternoon but decided later to walk in town during the early evening, when the sun had cooled down. The noise of the city was almost deafening. Everyone calling to everyone else. Movement all around us. Cars honking horns incessantly. At the butcher's alcove were hung skinned, sides of cow and lamb; no pork in this part of the world. The smells were as overwhelming as the noise. This was the Afghanistan which had existed for eons. Alive, pulsating, with everyone moving and talking and smoking; and then repeat. It was easy to get caught up in Kabul's night life.

Delhi

We arrived in Delhi the next day, after another two-hour flight. Like jumping on stones in a stream as we careened from Tehran to Kabul to Delhi. We were now in India, Sherry's father's birthplace. I could see that this visit was special for her. She was returning to one of the bedrocks of her existence. Using the Information Service at the airport, we found a hotel for our stay, the Vikram Hotel. It was smaller than others, but in our opinion, opulent in its finishings while in tune with my wallet. The Indian experience is sometimes soporific and other times overwhelming.

Again, it was very hot, which kept our activities to a minimum. The one-day trip we promised ourselves we would do was to take a pilgrimage to Agra to see the Taj Mahal. In a small Indian built car, we motored along the road to Agra, passing more adventurous and unpregnant tourists riding elephants. As much as I wanted to join the elephant herd, it would have been folly to try to talk Sherry into such a ride. We toot tooted along to Agra, hearing a horn blaring every second of the trip. National driving habits are easy to learn but not easy to accept. I guess Kabul imitated the Indian driving habits.

The Taj Mahal was and no doubt is one of the most extraordinary structures on the planet. The building itself is an ivory-white marble mausoleum, situated on the southern bank of the Yamuna River in the Indian city of Agra. It was commissioned in 1632 by the Mughal emperor, Shah Jahan (who reigned from 1628 to 1658), to house the tomb of his favourite wife, Mumtaz Mahal. It is also the resting place of Shah Jahan himself. The tomb is comprised of a 17-hectare (42-acre) complex, which includes a mosque and a guest house, and is set in formal gardens bounded on three sides by a crenelated wall.

We took photos from a distance, then closer, then next to the Taj Mahal itself. Those in prayer had left endless numbers of pairs of shoes outside the entrance to the mosque. The pattern of grounded shoes was itself settling. Even in the endless heat of an Indian summer's day. We found a place to sit under a tree, to rest in the heat and enjoy the world class spectacle in front of us. If

Sherry felt more special there because she is a Moslem, I don't recall. I just remember the beauty of the building and its ambiance, and the quiet and peaceful crowds enjoying the experience with us.

Lounging around the Vikram Hotel the next day, we saw an advertisement for a short holiday in Kashmir. Needless to say, neither of us had ever heard of Kashmir, so it wasn't on our "must do" list in India. When we talked to the concierge, he convinced us to visit Kashmir for a week. There was a special program for visiting Kashmir, and as we had no particular plans at this point of the trip, we decided to check it out. Lewis Carroll once wrote, "if you don't know where you are going, any road will get you there". We decided that the road to Kashmir was where we wanted to go.

Kashmir

The next morning we flew for ninety minutes from Delhi to Srinigar. Upon arrival, the travel agent had arranged for a taxi to meet us and drive to Dal Lake, northeast of the capital. The forty-five minute drive was non-eventful. We looked around us as we drove, watching how people in Kashmir lived. We soon arrived at the houseboat we had booked for a one-week holiday. The houseboat was staffed by three young men, who cooked, cleaned and arranged all of our other activities. The houseboat had three bedrooms, two more than we needed. The total cost per day for this opulence was ten US dollars. $10! Per day! Which Peace Corps Volunteer would refuse this option?

The day after our arrival, the resident three-man team suggested we go on a shikara, the flat-bottomed boats prevalent on Dal Lake; the gondolas of Kashmir. Our shikara was loaded with soft pillows, as in Kabul, on which we lay during each boat trip we took. Very comfortable for Sherry, given her condition. The shikara was covered with a cloth stretched over a wooden frame, to keep the intense sun from harming its occupants. The boatman can sit either in the front or at the back of the shikara. On different trips, our boatman sat both front and back. To move us about the Dal Lake, he used a five-foot-long oar, with a small, heart-shaped wooden paddle at the end. When he stroked with the oar, a beautiful water pattern was created behind us. Ripples moving in two directions away from the shikara. This was utter luxury. Lying on the large pillows, listening to the rippling water and the sounds from others on the lake, it was soporific.

Every day we went out in the shikara, sometimes just to journey around Dal Lake. Other times to see the large botanical gardens on the shores of Dal Lake, both Shalimar Bagh and Nishat Bagh. After disembarking the shikara, we walked around the fragrant and colourful gardens several times during our one-week visit.

We learned that many of the "islands" in the lake were built up from the vegetation of the lake. A boatsman would take a long pole and twist it around in the vegetation under water. He would bring up a pile of vegetation, dump it into a boat used for this purpose and let the vegetation dry. It takes many years but in time another island will be started by dumping the dry material into the lake and more and more similar materials on top of it. Eventually islands are created on which buildings can be built and people can live.

For a couple days, I sat on the top of the houseboat with a fishing pole and bait from our young gentlemen assistants and fished. Sitting in the middle of an amazing lake, on a clear summer's day, lazily and languishingly still fishing for whatever fish the lake would share with us. We ate what we caught on a couple nights while we were there.

On our way back to Delhi, we visited a carpet factory in Srinigar. While the carpet designs were made by older men, the actual weaving of the carpet was mainly done by children less than twelve years old. The carpets were not expensive, so we decided to buy a gold and white silk/wool carpet for three hundred dollars. We mailed it home from the factory and it was there waiting for us when we got to the US. It is still one of my prize possessions.

It was hard to leave our seventy-dollar week in Kashmir. The only negative during the week was the habit of our three boathouse gentlemen to all stand at attention in the narrow dining room at the ready every minute we were there. Inhibiting. Sherry wouldn't talk much as she didn't want them to hear our conversations. Our dining was more in silent mode than in joyous celebration. But leave we did, as we flew first to Delhi, where we packed up and headed for the next adventure: this time in Thailand.

Bangkok

The heat never abated. From Tehran to Kabul to Delhi to Kashmir to Thailand, the heat was intense. Sherry was more pregnant every day (that's how it works), and the heat made her tired much of the time. After settling into our hotel in Bangkok, the next morning was Sunday and I wanted to get out of the room. I went for a walk "around the block". What I didn't know about Bangkok is that a "block" in the city centre is very long. My walk around the block was close to a mile and a half and took some time. About ten minutes before I returned to the hotel, a young man, quite presentable, asked me in English how I was enjoying Bangkok. He wanted to know if I wanted to go see the "king's temple", which was the temple where the king had studied when he was a young boy. When we got to the hotel, he said he would wait outside while I went upstairs to convince Sherry to go with the young man and me to the king's temple.

Sherry was sceptical. She was cranky and didn't want to go out into the heat. But I was persistent and eventually she joined me. Her instincts were better than mine, as will be shown. We met the young man outside of the hotel, and were taken to a water taxi, one of the many which ply the Chao Phraya River. The water taxi is a narrow and long speedboat, with a very powerful engine on the back. We zipped over the waves at breakneck speed, every harrowing minute we were in this boat. Our guide tried to make all seem happy and relaxed but Sherry was not.

We ended up at two different temples. Each had a role (so the young man said), in the life of the king. Of course, at each temple there were the requisite buddhas, which one found everywhere in this lovely kingdom. Our guide spoke endlessly, tirelessly (for him) as he gave us an understanding of his country and its culture. After two hours in the hot sun, Sherry asked me to have him take us back to the hotel. Which he did. Until the middle of the Chao Phraya River, when the man operating the engine turned it off. I asked what happened and was told by my young friend that we had to pay an extra fifty dollars for the trip. Fifty dollars was like five thousand dollars for us, Peace Corps refugees lost in Thailand. When I refused and said we already had paid for the trip, he said if we didn't pay, he would throw us both out of the boat. And Sherry couldn't swim. Fortunately, I had fifty dollars on me. After we paid, he took us back to the port, and even paid for our taxi ride back to the hotel (which cost about twenty US cents). Sherry was shaken, livid and without words for the precarious position I had put her in. I could not argue with her.

The rest of the visit to Bangkok was a series of endless buddha visits. The golden buddha, the lying buddha, the standing buddha, the sitting buddha. A lifetime of buddha encounters all played out over a few days. Many of the buddhas were outstanding pieces of art and given their size, even overwhelming. I was particularly awed by the golden buddha which is located in the Wat Traimit temple. This six-ton statue was made around the 14th century but in the 18th century, was covered with plaster to prevent it from being noticed and stolen. Two hundred years later, in 1955, when the statue was being moved, it was dropped, the plaster cracked and a buddha made of gold valued at three hundred million dollars today appeared. The plasterer should be given the Dushdi Mala Medal (posthumously), the highest award one can receive in Thailand.

Taipei

We spent our last baht at the airport, as we prepared to board a flight to Taipei. It was an almost four-hour journey, long enough to be tiring. I had arranged to meet my boyhood friend and tennis partner, Wally, who was serving as a doctor in the Army in South Korea. He got drafted, something I had avoided by my Peace Corps stint. He took leave from his job in South Korea and flew to Taipei with his wife, Jackie, to meet Sherry and me for a mini-holiday together. But before we four met, Sherry and I had another pleasant activity to enjoy.

In my role as Treaties Officer in the Malawi Ministry of External Affairs, I had met with Ambassadors and other embassy staff of all of the embassies resident in Malawi. One of the most pleasant was the Ambassador from Taiwan, Ambassador Chen. I met with him frequently and got to know his number two, David Hong and wife Linda, very well. We socialized together frequently in Malawi. When we announced our plans in 1971 to visit

Taiwan on our way home, Ambassador Chen wrote a letter introducing us to his colleagues at home and arranged for us to have a lunch at the Ministry of Foreign Affairs in Taipei. Upon our arrival at the Ministry, we were treated like visiting dignitaries, meeting every official from the equivalent to the Permanent Secretary and down. The lunch they held in our honour, was long, delicious and full of warm words about the relationship between Malawi and Taiwan. It seemed a bit incongruous for me to be the Malawian representative at these meetings and lunch, but in the eyes of the Taiwanese, I was a Malawi Government official. They wanted to thank me and repay the many favours I showed to the Ambassador and the Hongs in Malawi while I worked at the Ministry of External Affairs. They also recommended and introduced me to a tennis club where I could play, and eventually did so with Wally after he arrived. We played two top players at that club.

The heat never abated. Across the sub-continent until we arrived in the Far East, it was a very hot summer, to the discomfort of Sherry and our unborn child. Nonetheless, I was looking forward to introducing Wally to Sherry. Wally was one of my closest high school friends. He and I had been tennis buddies for many years. We had participated together in several "pranks" on our friends, not all of which endeared us to them. Wally played a significant role in my teenage years and beyond and it was exciting for both of us to be meeting in a country so far from our suburban Chicago roots.

We stayed at a hotel recommended by Wally, who had PX privileges while in Taipei. During our stay, Wally and I played tennis at the local tennis club recommended by the Ministry of Foreign Affairs staff we met before. We enjoyed being outdoors and playing tennis together again. But we pretty much got hammered by the local talent.

The four of us drove one day to Taroko Gorge, one of the tourist attractions just outside of Taipei. It is located in the Taroko National Park. The Gorge, which includes a series of tunnels and turns through the mountainous countryside, is on the Liwu River. One tunnel had nine turns in it; we experienced from time to time views of the river and mountains in the distance as if we were watching the view on an Imax screen. A most pleasurable drive in a beautiful part of the country. The joy and wonder of Taroko Gorge was enjoyed while we drove in a car. Every so often we got out of the car at a viewing point and experienced the raw beauty of Taiwanese nature.

Our next tourist activity as a small group was more active, and very difficult for Sherry. It involved more than sitting in a car. We decided to visit the Bangka Lungshan Temple at the top of Elephant Mountain (Xiangshan). The Temple was originally reconstructed in 1738 and after several earthquakes, was rebuilt in 1924. Clambering up the more than five hundred steps in the heat and humidity of Taipei to reach the Temple was not easy. Sherry grumbled every step of the way; but somehow she made it to the top with the rest of us. The temple is more than a historical relic. It is an active place of worship. Unlike most temples one sees in Asia, Lungshan isn't affiliated with any major religion although unsurprisingly there were more buddhas to add to those we had seen in Thailand.

In the evenings we went to some of the many restaurants which are around the city. This was one of the few times on the trip that Sherry and I got to spend time with other people I knew. While some of the stories which Wally and I recounted to Sherry and Jackie were not much more than foolish high school jokes, recalling these events allowed us to leave the world we were traveling in and disappear into Wally's and my hazy juvenile memories. That and few beers helped to ease some of the stress that Sherry had experienced throughout the trip.

The departure date for Wally and Jackie came too soon. They went back to their South Korean life. Sherry and I decided to follow the recommendations from the people we met at the Ministry of Foreign Affairs and visit the famous Sun Moon Lake which is in Nantou County, in the centre of the country. It is the largest body of water in Taiwan. The area around the lake is home to the Thao tribe, one of aboriginal tribes of Taiwan. The east side of the lake resembles a sun while the west side resembles a moon, hence the name. Sun Moon Lake is located about 2,500 feet above sea level. The area surrounding the lake has many trails for hiking but given Sherry's condition and the memory of her five hundred step effort at Lungshan Temple, we rested most of the three days we were there, getting ready for the next leg of our endless journey.

Tokyo

The Japanese capital beckoned as we continued relentlessly with our Asian tour. Another airport, this time Haneda, outside of Tokyo. The almost three hour flight was uneventful. The ride into the city was slowed by heavy traffic. Our hotel for our stay in the Japanese capital was the Dai-Ichi Hotel, which was built in 1939 for the Olympics. It was a rectangular building, with not much to distinguish it from other rectangular buildings. The hotel met its fate in 2000 when it went bankrupt. Probably not a bad thing, given the rooms there.

We shared a room slightly bigger than the size of the bed. To walk past the bed, one of us had to get out of the way, either jump on the bed or go into the bathroom. It was the smallest room we stayed in during our trip back to the US. Some closets in other hotels on our trip had been bigger. This gave us an incentive to get out and about. Most of our travel in the city was by taxi, as taxis were ubiquitous. Because virtually no taxi driver spoke any language other than Japanese, we had to request the concierge to write our destination on a piece of paper to give to the driver each time we went out. And to keep a piece of paper with the hotel's name on it available for our return trips.

Fascinating to me were the restaurant offerings – in the windows. Plastic "meals" were shown to give potential customers an idea of what a particular meal looked like. Few were appetizing. I would imagine that some of those same "meals" continue to sit in the windows of the restaurants we visited.

One of our first trips outside of Tokyo was to Nikko, north of the city. There we found Toshogu, a 17th century shrine complex honouring the first shogun. It was in the mountains and heavily wooded, with cedar trees everywhere. A strong aroma like being in the inside of an old closet. The main gate was magnificent, as were the temples in the complex. It was a warm, August day, with crowds of people everywhere. One advantage over the heat of an August day in Tokyo was the mountain air, cooler, and of course cedarly. We spent an afternoon at the shrine in Nikko, before heading back to our postage-stamp sized hotel room.

The next day we travelled to Nara, by way of Mt. Fuji. We took a tour, riding on a bullet train (150 miles per hour). At Mt. Fuji, we all got out to see the mountain. Or a part of it as it was cloudy that day and only parts of the mountain were visible. We had a lunch with our tour group and then returned to the train for the ride to Nara.

During my senior year at the University of Wisconsin, I took a course on Japanese gardens. That is when I was first observed the wonder and glory of these famed areas of vegetation. There are many gardens in Nara but I remember the Chikurin-in Temple and Garden there. We also visited the Jikoin Temple where we enjoyed not only the amazing gardens, but also some matcha tea. I gave Sherry a lecture on the symbolism in Japanese gardens as I had studied some from Nara during my university studies. Not sure she was that interested as her growing tummy made travel more and more difficult for her.

Finally, our Asian tour was over. We had to leave Japan. We had booked a ship that went from Yokohama to Honolulu. This was to be an eight day adventure on the all first class cabin SS President Wilson, which was part of the American President Lines. The ship had been launched just after the end of World War II, as it had intended to be a troop carrier. It was refurbished into a luxury cruise ship, on which every passenger could access every deck. We didn't know it at the time, but within a couple years, the ship was de-commissioned and taken out of service. Only our memories remain of this wonderful ship. Those memories and our trip back to the US and eventually to our Washington, D.C. home (and Samantha's birth) will be the subject of another story.

Completed: April 11, 2024

THE BIRTH AND DEATH OF SARTOC

Aleke Banda. (A-Lay-Kay). The youngest Minister at the birth of Malawi. Imprisoned in Rhodesia in 1959 with his namesake, Dr. Hastings Kamuzu Banda, eventually the President of the Republic of Malawi. Aleke was Minister of Finance and also Minister of Commerce & Industry when the Department of Tourism was formed under his tutelage in 1962. Later Aleke was appointed Minister of Information & Tourism, the first time that tourism had its own Minister. He served as the Chairman of Air Malawi after Central African Airways fell apart at the end of 1967. Tourism and Aleke are inextricably tied to each other in the early history of Malawi.

It all started with Aleke. As so many things did. He was young, intelligent and spirited. He wanted everything to happen yesterday. His small stature and overpowering smile were deceptive. Aleke knew what he was doing and where he wanted Malawi to go. His confidence was an indication that the new generation of Malawian leaders would show the former colonial masters that the country was in safe hands. In the pursuit of his interests, Aleke was given wide latitude by President Banda, as he was one of his favourite Ministers. So how did I get involved with Aleke and eventually SARTOC?

Treaties Officer

I began working as Treaties Officer in the Ministry of External Affairs on December 1, 1968, upon my return from three weeks of holiday after finishing my Peace Corps stint. It was in this guise that I was brought into the Aleke orbit. For most of 1968, I was undecided about what I would do after completing my two-year Peace Corps assignment in Malawi at the end of that year. I considered options such as a trip through West Africa with Eddie (my law school roommate who had been teaching as a Peace Corps Volunteer in Liberia), studying for a Masters degree at the School of Oriental and African Studies (SOAS) at the University of London where my application had just been accepted, or a trip through Europe and the UK. After meeting Sherry in May of 1968 at a Lions Club fete, all these plans went up in smoke.

One of my friends in Blantyre was Hank, an American lawyer who had graduated from Yale and was advising the Malawi Government as Treaties Officer in its Ministry of External Affairs. Hank was one of six American lawyers in Malawi from Syracuse University's Maxwell Program. Each of these lawyers worked in different Ministries in Blantyre, Lilongwe and Zomba. Hank played a lot of basketball with many of my Peace Corps colleagues, and it was through sport that we first met. He informed me in late summer 1968 that he was finishing his contract in October and suggested that I consider taking over from him.

It wasn't only Hank who was pleading my case. Sherry and I started dating in July 1968, initially on July 6th, Republic Day, when she accepted my invitation to attend the festivities as Mrs Friedlander. This was because the written invitation I received for the Celebrations was addressed to Mr and Mrs Friedlander. Her roommate in Blantyre was Debra, a South African who was in a romantic relationship with John, the Permanent Secretary in the Ministry of External Affairs. John had a strong belief that Malawi should wean itself away from English advisers and instead find and use American advisers. Hank was actually the second American to help John's Ministry as Treaties Officer. Before Hank, an American named Jerry held the same position in the Ministry. Through Debra, I was introduced to John. After John described to me what Hank had been doing for his Ministry, I told him that I would be interested in applying for the post of Treaties Officer when my Peace Corps contract was over.

Of course it wasn't as simple as that. It never is. As I was a licensed lawyer (albeit only in Illinois), the track to Treaties Officer required me to be first hired by the Attorney General, Bryan Roberts, easily the most powerful man in the country after President Banda. I would then be seconded from the Attorney General's Chambers in Zomba to the Ministry of External Affairs in Blantyre. To accomplish this, I had to be interviewed by the Malawi Public Service Commission (PSC), as all such appointments required the PSC interview and recommendation. This was arranged sometime in the early Fall, when I attended a PSC meeting with four of its members: one English lawyer and one New Zealand lawyer from the Attorney General's Chambers and two Malawian PSC members.

I found a suit and tie from somewhere to wear for the interview. This was one of the first job interviews I had ever had and I was anxious about my chances of surviving an interrogation from the PSC. These anxieties faded after the first question: where had I gone to law school? I could tell when I mentioned Harvard Law School that the interview was over. Maybe John had helped guide the PSC through my interview but having attended a law school that they had all heard of may have been the deciding factor. I was learning – what's in a name?

Air Services Agreements

As soon as I started working in the Ministry of External Affairs in December 1968, I attended meetings and met with many members of the civil service working for the Malawi Government. One of the Ministries that was most active internationally was the Ministry of Transport & Communications, along with its counterpart, the Civil Aviation Authority. Air Malawi had been formed in 1964, as one of the country's first strides into Independence. Air Malawi was initially a subsidiary of Central African Airways (CAA). But at the end of 1967, CAA was liquidated and Malawi, Rhodesia and Zambia, the three participants in the CAA, each began operating their own airlines.

Air Malawi's fleet originally consisted of DC-3s only. These were mainly for internal and a couple regional flights. But with Aleke in charge, the airline started to grow, to show its wings to the world. Instead of having only regional routes, the plan was to establish long-haul routes to places like Ethiopia, Cyprus and the ultimate landing place, London. The first planes bought by Air Malawi were the HS-748 and the Britten-Norman Islander. Soon after the BAC-111 was added. All were for local and regional flights. Its first long-haul aircraft, the VC-10, was leased by Air Malawi in 1972. However, having a long-haul aircraft was the last step in a process that began with the negotiation of air services agreements with countries through which such aircraft would land, discharge and pick up passengers. Air services agreements are usually more than fifty-pages long and of course took time to draft and negotiate and even more time to implement.

That's when I first met Aleke, as part of the air services agreement negotiation team which included the General Manager of Air Malawi, the head of the Civil Aviation Authority and officials from the Ministries of Transportation and Finance. The first meetings with him were dynamic, charged with energy and a sense of purpose. The experienced air services heads were a South African man at Air Malawi and of course a British man at the Civil Aviation Authority. Each had endless years of experience in air services in Africa. The Malawian civil servant participants and I were the neophytes. No place to go but up. Literally.

The process of negotiating an air services agreement revealed the limited resources we had available in the Ministry to provide advisory services to the Malawi Government. I had a secretary, Avril, a young, blond Irish lass who was an excellent organizer and typist. But she had to suffer through the months of drafting which preceded direct negotiations. Aleke wanted us to have our own model air services agreement so I had to prepare one from scratch without knowing much about the industry. With a bit of support from the so-called library in my office, really one shelf with a few books on international law, I wrote by hand the full fifty-page document. Avril readily typed what I wrote, although she failed many times to decipher my hasty and nervously scripted draft.

The technology of the time required one to prepare a stencil, from which many copies could be made. When an error was made in the draft stencil, it had to be filled with a red liquid and when it dried, the revised letters were typed over the earlier mistakes. This also meant I had to proofread every word of every page that Avril typed. This process was difficult enough, but got worse when the other country decided to add a paragraph or two in the middle of the document. This meant that Avril would not only have to prepare the stencil with the new wording, she would also have to re-type all the pages that appeared after the new wording, so that the document would appear seamless. And once again I had to proofread everything. When I think back to this process, I wonder how we ever got anything done correctly. Our success was certainly more due to Avril than myself.

Negotiations in Cyprus

The first international trip I took as a member of the air services agreement negotiation team of the Malawi Government was to Cyprus in 1969. This was five years before the Turks invaded the northern part of the country. We stayed in Nicosia, which was the capital of Cyprus at the time, but which later fell under Turkish rule. All negotiations were held in Nicosia. As part of our negotiations, we were also encouraged to see much of this beautiful island as tourists. One day, we went to Kyrenia for lunch, a colourful port town with a secluded, semi-circular bay of deep blue water and buildings of endless pastels and white which contrasted with the bright yellow sun and the blue of the sea. Kyrenia was a painting, and its attractive bayside villas were some of the most expensive in the country. Eating at an outdoor café, quaffing a glass of wine and taking in the ambiance of this amazing corner of Cyprus was one of the highlights of the trip. We then drove on to Famagusta, with its old churches and castles and other ruins, before returning to our Nicosia base. A most beautiful country, headed at the time by Archbishop Makarios, an international figure of note. He was not only the patriarch of the Church but also the President of the country.A modern Henry VIII.

The Cyprus negotiating team was experienced, all much older than I was. In sync with the mode of the time, it was also all male. Due to its location in the Mediterranean Sea, many countries had negotiated air services agreements with Cyprus. They were a serious and formidable negotiating team. But they were also decent people and very accommodating to the young Malawi Government's efforts to enter the international, long-haul air services market. The crux of the air services agreement on the table was the negotiation of so-called Fifth Freedom rights, which allowed Air Malawi to discharge passengers in, and pick up passengers from, Cyprus.

One advantage to our negotiations in Cyprus was that they had a team of typists, not just lonely Avril, who could work on all aspects of the agreement at the same time. So each day's negotiations resulted in new documents the next morning updating all of us on the status of the draft as of the day before. At the end of the week-long negotiations, the head of the Cyprus negotiating team gave a toast to the visiting Malawi delegation. He thanked us for the seriousness of our negotiations and announced that the draft we had finally agreed upon the day before would become the basis of all further air services agreement negotiations for the Cyprus Government. Our small team had helped to lay down a mark in the history of Cypriot air services documentation.

Negotiations in Ethiopia

A year later found our team in Addis Ababa, Ethiopia. This was an important link in Air Malawi's plan to have air services to Europe and eventually London. Air Malawi would either fly through Cyprus or Addis Ababa or both on its way to London. I have always loved visiting Addis Ababa, as its location in the high hills of southern Ethiopia is quite unlike any other place in southern Africa. Addis Ababa is almost eight thousand feet above sea level. During the first couple days after arrival, one can tire easily. At certain times of the year, the city is bitterly cold during the day. This despite the "thirteen months of sunshine" which is the country's tourism mantra.

The negotiating team for Ethiopian Airlines and the Ethiopian Government was much younger, or at least looked so, than the team we had met in Cyprus. Similar to the Cyprus team, they were all male. This was not a time when women would be found in leading positions in the civil service in Africa. The entire team was Ethiopian which was quite different from our expatriate-heavy Malawi Government team. Ethiopian Airlines was formed in 1945, and from the beginning had a special relationship with TransWorld Airlines (TWA). It began long-haul flights in the 1950s. In 1964, TWA developed, erected and managed a six million dollar aircraft and engine service facility in Addis Ababa so that Ethiopian Airlines could service aircraft of other airlines in Africa and the Middle East.

The proud tradition of Ethiopian Airlines was apparent during our negotiations. The younger members of the Ethiopian team were all university educated outside of Ethiopia. They were intelligent, smart-looking, well-spoken -- the vanguard of African youth of the future. The negotiations were also intermixed with tourism adventures as we were taken around Addis Ababa, driven southeast to Debre Zeyit and visited other outlying areas. I will never forget seeing the lions in Emperor Haile Selassie's gated palace gardens in the centre of Addis Ababa, smaller and darker than their game park cousins in East and Southern Africa, but a direct symbol of the power and endurance of the Emperor. Four years later, that endurance would be tested as the Emperor's world was torn asunder.

By the end of the week, we had negotiated another successful air services agreement which would allow Air Malawi to exercise its Fifth Freedom rights to discharge and pick up passengers in Addis Ababa when its as yet unavailable aircraft travelled from Malawi to Europe and back to Malawi. On our final night, we had a party with our Ethiopian colleagues which was full of clicking champagne glasses, canapes and lovely words about each other's countries. I cannot forget the promise for the future of the country that presented itself in the persons of the young and gifted Ethiopian team. I never learned what happened to my dear friends on September 12, 1974 when the Derg overturned Ethiopia in ways no one could ever imagine. They would have been targets for the topsy-turvy weltanschauung of Col. Mengistu Haile-Mariam, the head of the Derg and leader of the Revolution.

Birth of SARTOC

Today if I mention in Malawi or anywhere in southern Africa the Southern African Regional Tourism Council (SARTOC), not a head will turn, not an eye will blink, not a soul will confirm that this entity ever existed. But it did. At the instigation of Aleke of course. Probably he sold this idea to President Banda. It was the type of action that Aleke would have initiated. On August 3, 1970, a five-day conference on regional tourism co-operation was opened in Blantyre. The participants at the conference were government ministerial representatives from Lesotho, Malawi, Mauritius, Portugal (on behalf of Angola and Mozambique – yes, still under Portuguese rule), South Africa and Swaziland.

One of the members of the Mauritius delegation was Regis, the Director of Tourism for this small, yet glamorous island nation located east of Madagascar in the Indian Ocean. As a result of his attending the conference, Regis and I became lifelong friends. Regis was of mixed French and Indian descent. He was married to an English woman, Margaret. They lived in a lovely old home in Rose Hill with their three energetic and bright children. When Sherry and I started our round-the-world tour in June 1971 after leaving Malawi, our first stop was in Mauritius because Regis insisted that we visit him and his family. Regis and Margaret gave us their bedroom for our week-long visit to Mauritius. We visited every tourist site in the country in this short period, and even had tea with the Prime Minister of Mauritius on a Sunday afternoon before we left. Our stay in Mauritius is captured in another short story.

During the August 1970 conference, discussions were held at various tourism destinations in Malawi, beginning with the self-proclaimed international standard Mt. Soche Hotel in Blantyre which had first opened its doors in 1969. It was here that the conference officially began when President Banda gave the opening speech on August 4, 1970. After another day of discussions at the Mt. Soche Hotel, the participants drove up to Club Makokola, a new beach hotel in the Fort Johnston area. Here the participants relaxed on the golden sands of the beach and in the warm, blue waters of Lake Malawi while meeting in informal groups to continue discussions on the promotion of tourism in southern Africa. The informal beach atmosphere was conducive to the development of personal relationships between the participants, even with South Africa and Portugal in attendance.

Another of the tourism activities served up to conference participants was a daytime lake cruise on the *Ilala II*, the largest ship on Lake Malawi. During the several hour cruise on a bright August day, several of us played shuffleboard on the deck of the ship while sipping cordials and Carlsberg Beer, a local beer brand from Malawi's only international brewery. The smooth sailing ship was the perfect venue for the participants to bond with other tourism experts from the same region of Africa.

During the conference, each country representative made a presentation about the existing and proposed tourism development activities in his country. After each presentation was made, it was reviewed and discussed by the conference as a whole. These discussions gave each country an inside view of where the other countries were going with their tourism developments and investments. On the last day of the conference, in support of Aleke's grand plan, it was decided by the conference in plenary session that a regional tourism authority should be established to promote and coordinate tourism development in the Southern African region. All parties agreed to meet again in Malawi in early 1971 to begin the steps required for the legal formation of this body. This was the body that would eventually be known as SARTOC.

In February of 1971, lawyers representing each of the countries that had participated in the August 1970 conference met in Blantyre. The basis for negotiations was the draft articles of association which had been prepared by myself and other members of the Malawi

Government. It took most of a week for the attendees to finalize and approve the draft articles of association of SARTOC. Aleke was proud that Malawi had been the mover and shaker of tourism cooperation amongst southern African countries.

A press release from February 24, 1971 tells the story of the meeting of legal minds: "It was agreed to recommend to their respective Governments that a Southern African Regional Tourism Council, to be known as SARTOC, be established. The main objective of SARTOC, which it is hoped will be in operation in the near future, is to promote and develop, through regional co-operation, the tourism industry in the Southern African Region, which includes the islands of the Indian Ocean. The seat of SARTOC will be in Malawi, and it is hoped that the inaugural meeting of SARTOC will be held in Mauritius."

The SARTOC articles of agreement were signed by South Africa on August 19, 1971, during the State visit of President Banda to the Republic of South Africa. The articles of agreement were to come into force when signed by four States. As of August 1971 the articles of association were signed by Malawi, South Africa and Swaziland. The fourth country to sign the articles of association was Mauritius. SARTOC was born. Another feather in Aleke's cap. He was very proud of this newly born international baby.

It took time before this new organization found its feet. Office space was needed and its first staff members recruited. An executive director needed to be recruited and appointed. The Department of Tourism was the logical source of manpower in Malawi, but every person recruited to SARTOC from Malawi would reduce the capabilities of its own Department of Tourism. An international solution was required. It came in 1973 in the person of Frank who had arrived in Malawi in September 1972 to serve as Senior Tourism Officer in the Department of Tourism. It took less than a year for Frank to be appointed the first Executive Director of SARTOC, a most fortuitous choice.

Frank had tourism in his blood. He had worked in the tourism department of the Republic of Cyprus in London before coming to Malawi, bringing strong credentials to his new job. Frank had just turned thirty years of age, was fair-haired, 6'6", lanky, lean, with a gregarious smile and a sprightly Irish sense of humour. Frank was born in Northern Ireland and met his Argentinian wife, Maria, in Manchester in 1964. He arrived in Malawi in 1972 with Maria, and two small kids. He brought the enthusiasm of a young man to the post, and in the course of the rest of his life in Malawi, a love for Malawi which was stronger than that of most born in the country. In 1974, Frank introduced the tagline which has become the watchword of Malawi tourism: "The Warm Heart of Africa". Every Malawi tourism publication since then has had the "warm heart of Africa" on its front or back, burned into the memory of all who have visited the country. It even became the title of a book about the Peace Corps experiences of Jack in Balaka in the late 1960s, although the term didn't exist when Jack lived in Malawi.

Frank had an Oxford education and a relentless curiosity about Malawi and the people who made the history of the country. His tourism adventures included his tour in the Ministry and being Executive Director of SARTOC. Later he and Ambassador Jake, one of Malawi's most engaging representatives abroad, formed a consulting partnership to advise Malawian entities on tourism related projects, including in the aviation industry.

His interest in Africana books led him into being one of the largest collectors of such books on the continent. Eventually he started publishing books on various aspects of Malawi, including birds, history and tourism adventures. His publishing capabilities included the annual reports of Malawi corporate and parastatal entities, which brought Frank closer to those in power in the country. His disdain for negligence, sloppiness and intentional wrongs never waned. For this reason, his direct observations were not always welcomed. Frank was not Don Quixote tilting at windmills; he was a sophisticated observer of Malawian politics and people, but he never let these thoughts go beyond his close personal relationships.

Sadly and unexpectedly, Frank had a stroke in mid-December of 2020, and passed away two days before Christmas. His family and friends were devastated, including myself. But even more, Malawi lost a lover of art, photography, history and politics who will no longer be able to observe, comment and help to steer Malawi away from the abyss.

Death of SARTOC

In the end, the ideas behind the formation of SARTOC were shared by too few countries. If the seven original participants had all signed up to the SARTOC concept and more importantly funded it, perhaps SARTOC would be still alive today. But with only Malawi, Mauritius, Swaziland and South Africa as members, over time SARTOC became dependent on the South African capital contribution to the organization. This meant that its policies and interests of SARTOC had to mirror those of South Africa. That was not the intention when Aleke first came up with his idea for regional tourism cooperation. He wanted Malawi to take a leading role in a new regional organization, and to keep punching above its weight in the tourism sector, which might lead to more authority elsewhere in the region.

Frank was sanguine about the collapse of SARTOC. His Executive Directorship had lasted long after its "use by" date. Internal politics and a meagre budget restricted his ability to take the organization where he thought it should be. Because the organization never grew beyond the original four countries, the ability to design and operate regional tourism development plans was weakened and eventually stifled. SARTOC is gone; Aleke is gone; and now, Frank is gone. And covid is here, making regional tourism more a dream than a reality. The birth of tourism in Malawi is over but the contributions of those who had the vision and desire to develop Malawi's tourism resources and promote regional tourism in southern Africa will never be forgotten, especially in the "Warm Heart of Africa".

Completed: February 20, 2021

GOING FOR GOLD

Peter

It all began with Peter, my dear friend Peter. A South African working at the World Bank, with an American wife and six delightful kids. His father was a mining engineer. Peter's job was to structure and implement mining and industrial projects at the World Bank. We first met in 1972 when I joined the World Bank's Legal Department. Peter and I were both active in the formation and first iteration of the World Bank Staff Association, which breathed its first in September 1972. We served together on the Executive Committee of the Staff Association in its formative days and beyond.

Before Peter resigned from the Bank in 1974 to establish his own consulting firm, he was my most active and persistent supporter for my eventual candidacy for the position of Chairman of the Staff Association. I was hesitant. It was not in my character or experience to seek an office of this level of exposure and importance. Nor had I spent any time in the past as an activist fighting the powers that be. I was a faithful if restless member of the Legal Department and provided my legal services as needed to the countries to which I was eventually assigned. The Staff Association provided spice to the grist of the daily World Bank routine. At the end of 1973, Peter lobbied me for months to put my hat in the ring as a candidate for the position of Chairman. I eventually succumbed, ran for and was elected Chairman in 1974, but that story is not relevant now.

Because of my African experience prior to joining the Bank, Peter introduced me to Ernie, an experienced, world-class geologist based in Minneapolis. He was thoughtful and deliberate in all he did, and best of all, seemed to know the scope and details of every deposit of every mineral in the world. All this from a Minneapolis base at a time where the internet was neither a word nor a reality.

Citibank

After I left the World Bank in 1975, I joined the Nairobi, Kenya office of First National City Bank of New York (a year later it morphed into Citibank). My expectations for a long career in Citibank ended when management wanted to send me to Lagos, Nigeria in 1978 as head of the Bank's office there. It was an honour to be selected to run a Citibank branch overseas, especially with the little banking experience I had at that time. But Citibank did not yet have a licenced branch as the Nigerian Government refused to issue Citibank a banking license unless Nigerian citizens owned forty percent of the local legal entity. According to my boss, Bob, Citibank never opened a bank in a country unless it owned one hundred percent of the equity. As it turned out, Citibank and the Nigerian Government didn't agree on this issue until 1984, long in the future, when Citibank finally opened its first Lagos office – with minority Nigerian partners.

So I left Citibank and joined the new Kenya-based office of the Washington, DC law firm, Duncan, Allen and Mitchell, in January 1978. Our office was about two hundred meters from the Citibank office, so this career move didn't affect my living or family situation much. Duncan, Allen and Mitchell already had offices in Kinshasa, Zaire and Abidjan, Ivory Coast, so Nairobi gave us the third lynchpin across the middle of Africa, like the stars that comprise Orion's belt: Alnilam (Abidjan), Alnitak (Kinshasa) and Mintaka (Nairobi). At this time, we were the only American law firm with offices in Africa. With the flood of American lawyers running around Africa these days, it is wistful to remember how lonely our little flags were in the three countries we called home. We had broken significant ground to establish a legal presence in Africa and the associated branding necessary to compete in these markets, both with local and offshore legal service providers.

As 1980 approached, Peter was hired as a consultant to assist on a mining project in Ghana. He suggested that I visit the country, as there would be opportunities for legal services in connection with the project on which he was working. At that time, my close Malawian friend, Charles, was Country Head of the World Bank office in Accra. I contacted Charles and he encouraged me to come to Accra and stay with his family while there.

First Visit to Ghana

Charles was the first Malawian to serve as a permanent secretary in any Malawi Government ministry, a lofty position indeed. Charles was the Jackie Robinson of the Malawi civil service. He had a few assignments as permanent secretary, with his first in the Ministry of Health. I started working for the Ministry of External Affairs of the Malawi Government in December 1968. Before I left in June 1971, Charles and I became close friends. While I was still at the Ministry of External Affairs, Charles got himself into a bit of pickle, I think because the British establishment was not yet supportive of promoting young Malawians to such senior positions. He was accused of some long-forgotten impropriety. For some reason, the Malawi Government decided to remove him from the country in a nice way, as opposed to what had been done in other cases, and helped Charles to apply for and obtain a position at the World Bank. Charles accepted this largesse and ended up in Washington, DC at some point in 1971.

After a visit to Duncan, Allen and Mitchell's Abidjan office near the end of 1979, I boarded a Ghana Airways flight to Accra, a short, one-hour hop from Francophone to Anglophone Africa. Thankfully, only one hour. Because I booked the flight at the last minute, I could only get a middle seat in economy class. I had no idea that I would be sitting between two wonderful Ghanaian market women who had travelled to Abidjan to buy goods unavailable in Ghana and were now on their way back home. Both of these ladies were full of laughter and good spirit. Both were also of Ghanaian market women proportions, which left me little room in the middle seat. Very little room. I could lie and claim I held my breath for one hour, but that would be seen for what it is. Instead, I found a way to sit at an angle so that I could continue breathing, while engaging with the two gregarious women who were my row-mates.

While in Abidjan, I was unable to obtain a visa to visit Ghana. I was told this is not a problem as visas were issued upon arrival at the airport. The heat of a Ghanaian afternoon greeted me as I descended the stairs to the tarmac of Kotoka International Airport. It was a short walk to a one-story building which served as the terminal. Along with the other passengers, I walked down a long corridor before we got to the Immigration desks. As I had no visa, I had to wait until all the other passengers were admitted into the country. Then an immigration officer asked me to come with him to get my visa. We walked about half way back down the long corridor. He opened a door on the left. In this room sat a wooden desk, and two chairs, one for him and one for me. I was a bit apprehensive.

I sat down in front of him and asked how I could obtain a visa. He said it was no problem; the cost was five American dollars. Feeling more assured and relieved, I filled out an entry form, and gave it to him. I also handed him a five-dollar bill. He opened a drawer in the desk and threw the bill into a drawer which was littered with bills of many currencies: British pounds, French francs, Japanese yen, Deutsche marks, a cornucopia of paper money. The drawer was filled almost to the top, without organization but definitely with purpose. He took my passport, stamped a visa on one of the pages, handed me the passport, and wished me a pleasant stay in Ghana. No receipt for the five dollars was offered; I assumed it was not politic to ask for one. With my newly acquired visa in hand, I walked back to the Immigration desk, proudly showed my visa to the officer and with the loud bang of a stamp in my passport, I was granted entry into the Ghanaian capital.

I stayed with Charles and his family for a couple days. He drove me around Accra, showed me all the places that tourists see. We went to the beach one day. We relived our days in Malawi and chatted much about his job, his view of the World Bank (particularly his role as country manager), and what he wanted to do in the future. For Charles, the job in Ghana was a way to make some extra money and also a stepping stone to a better job back at headquarters in DC. It was a pleasure to share some time with a good friend in a foreign environment.

Gold Promotion Council

After I returned to Nairobi, I contacted Peter who arranged for me to be invited to join his team which was going to be retained to advise the Ghana Government on the revitalization of its gold sector. The UN contracting entity for the project was UNDP, the United Nations Development Program, the UN entity based in New York with a mandate to assist developing countries around the world with their development activities. In 1979, a study of the Ghana State Gold Mines at Tarkwa and Dunkwa was carried out by the UN, UNDP and the Ghana Government. It was this report which led to the establishment of the Gold Promotion Council (GPC) in Ghana. The report's main findings were directed at the lowering of gold production in Ghana from one million ounces at Independence to three hundred thousand ounces in 1979. In 2016, Ghana produced over four million ounces, so maybe the efforts of the GPC almost forty years before eventually came to fruition.

The then Vice President of Ghana, Dr. Joseph de Graft-Johnson, was appointed head of the newly formed GPC. He was one of founders of the Popular Front Party (PFP), the main opposition to the Peoples National Party (PNP). In 1979 the PNP's candidate, Hilla Limann, was elected president. Dr. Johnson was the first person to be appointed to the position of vice president in Ghana. It was only a couple months before I found myself back in Ghana in 1980, as a member of the GPC team.

For this assignment, we stayed at the then Continental Hotel in Accra, about a seven minute drive from the airport. In 1980 it was an older hotel, faded from its earlier glory, if ever. While the service in the hotel, mainly male waiters who had worked there for decades, was outstanding, the physical plant of the hotel had suffered with the inexorable passing of time and the concomitant lack of maintenance. The rooms looked old, tired and less graceful than when they were first conceived. No wifi was necessary; it was 1980! The hotel has since been taken over by the Golden Tulip Hotel group and renovated to a five-star standard.

We and our Ghanaian counterparts in the GPC operated from an office in the Ministry of Finance, up on the second floor. It was an old, colonial office building which had seen better days. Each office had its own air conditioner, a mandatory piece of equipment in a country located just north of the Equator and riding the Atlantic Ocean. Along with the loud, squeaky and dripping air conditioner in our office, which only worked when electricity was flowing, were the usual multi-coloured, water streaked walls, inside and outside, commonly present in buildings in tropical climates. Yet, even with the air conditioning at full blast, the humidity caused clothes to stick to skin. More ubiquitous than the air conditioners were the various-sized green, brown and gray geckos which dotted the walls, floors and mysteriously, walked fearlessly on the ceiling. These were the protectors of the realm, gobbling up every flying and walking insect which had the gall to inhabit our space.

Our main local contact at the GPC on a day-to-day basis was Ben, who had been trained as an economist. While not on his list of responsibilities to the team, Ben enjoyed taking time to educate and enlighten Peter and myself on Ghanaian culture, language and customs. This was often done during our daily lunch breaks, when we went outside to buy plantains and peanuts from roadside vendors and sat in the shade where Ben would wax warmly about the various aspects of Ghana that we needed to know to perform our roles. Naturally Ben's political and socialistic leanings manifested themselves as we talked. For both Peter and myself, Ben played an important part in making sure that our work was relevant to Ghanaian society and norms.

The more perfunctory obligations placed on Ben's shoulders were the making of appointments in Accra with the various stakeholders whom we were asked to approach in carrying out our advisory role for GPC. Later he also organized a trip we made to the four major Government-owned and operated gold mining operations in Ghana at that time, at Tarkwa, Dunkwa, Prestea and Obuasi.

Mining in Zambia

I was excited to work with Peter and the GPC team in Ghana. I got into the mining business in Africa at the end of 1975, when I started working for Citibank in Nairobi. My first two clients at Citibank were the copper/cobalt mining giants of Zambia, Roan Consolidated Mines (RCM), and Nchanga Consolidated Copper Mines (NCCM). RCM was established in 1928 by the Roan Selection Trust of South Africa. NCCM was established shortly after in 1931 by Anglo-American's Rhodesian operations. After Independence in 1964, the Zambian government decided it wanted a bigger share of the mining pie. So, both companies were partially nationalized in 1969 when fifty-one percent (51%) of the shares of each company were transferred to the socialist-leaning government of Kenneth Kaunda. Not the best decision ever made by Kaunda or his government.

Both RCM and NCCM had several mining operations in the country. RCM had underground mines at Mufulira and Luanshya. NCCM was best known for its largest asset, the Nchanga open pit, one of the world's largest open pit copper mines. Before the end of 1976, I had visited all of these mining operations while performing the role of lead banker from Citibank to Zambia and the Zambian copper/cobalt industry.

Mining in Ghana

I was anxious to see how the gold mining business in Ghana differed from the copper/cobalt mining businesses which I knew well in Zambia. Ben organized our upcoming trip through the gold mines of Ghana. Our "gold swing" in 1980 turned out to be quite the trip. Our first stop was Takoradi, not a mine itself but the main port through which imports into and exports from the mining industry flowed. The trip to Takoradi should have taken five hours, but Ben had gone to a college at Cape Coast, which was on the way to Takoradi, and he wanted to stop and visit friends there. Peter and I were happy to see more of the country, so the stop at Cape

Coast was a welcome break. Ben met some of his former teachers, while we ambled in the ambiance of the college. Soon we were on the way to the port of Takoradi.

What can one say about a port? There are ships and cranes all around, and many people either working hard or hardly working. We walked down the long pier, asked some questions, getting a feeling for the port. We didn't stay long as we had to travel to the mine at Tarkwa, where we would spend the night. At the roundabout outside the port where we turned north to Tarkwa, we saw people filling potholes in the road. The Ghana Government of the day had started a self-help program through which local citizens had responsibilities for keeping the roads where they lived in working shape. A dozen or so men were making sure the potholes disappeared, at least for the moment. The next heavy rain would probably undo these efforts.

Tarkwa

Our visit to Tarkwa was harrowing, to say the least. After a good night's sleep, we went to the mine to meet senior management. At that time, the mine at Tarkwa was going through the same financial and economic pressures that affected the entire Ghanaian economy. Little money was available for operation and maintenance of the mine; even less for development. Mining at Tarkwa today is done through open pit operations. This was not true in 1980, when a shaft was required to reach the area of underground mining.

We were taken to the one operating shaft for a trip to the depths of the mine. We were told that maintenance on the cage and hoist of the shaft was not up to date. This caused much discussion among the GPC advisors, especially by Peter and myself. After being given a choice to descend or stay at the top, we made the decision to descend in a rickety, noisy and less than stable cage. A long ride down, down, down into the bowels of the earth. With many silent prayers from some of us. We finally reached the level where the majority of mining operations were taking place.

The ore body at Tarkwa consisted of a series of sedimentary banket quartz reef units similar to those mined in the Witwatersrand Basin of South Africa. The heat and humidity were almost overwhelming as we stepped gratefully out of the swinging cage, almost into a pool of water. While the descent reminded me somewhat of my descent in an RCM mine in Zambia, it was clear that operations at Tarkwa were less controlled, much more haphazard.

Extending away from where we left the cage were rail tracks. Cars were used to haul the mined ore from the area of operations to a central point for removal to the surface. We rode in a car for ten minutes and then walked a short time before we reached the area where mining operations were taking place. The conditions were oppressive, as sweat appeared everywhere it can. We talked to the miners as they carried out their duties and learned about the issues they faced. The thought of working for eight hours a day in these conditions was not pleasant. For us, a short trip into mining hell; for them, it was their lives and livelihood. I decided then and there that I didn't want to be a miner.

Dunkwa

The next stop on our tour was Dunkwa, an alluvial mining site on the Ofin River. This was the only gold mine we would visit without a shaft penetrating into the earth to the gold deposits. Instead, mining was done by a dredge on the river as it had been for at least eighty years. The dredge we mounted was recently purchased from a manufacturer in Scotland by the Ghana State Gold Mining Corporation for £4.2 million. It was state-of-the-art; so we were told.

The dredge pulled up earth and water from the river bank and the river bed by a conveyer belt of buckets, spaced about a yard apart. As the belt turned, the buckets dug into the river bank or bed and dumped its contents into a large concentrator on the dredge itself. Water was removed and the remaining gold-bearing earth was treated through several processes to end up as a concentrate with a profitable, recoverable percentage of gold.

One could easily see where the dredge's operations had eaten into the river bank. It was not a pretty sight. But it was effective. The dredge had a lighting system so it could operate twenty-four hours a day, although I am not sure that they achieved this capability very often. There were not that many "miners" working that day as our visiting group doubled the number of men on the dredge. No women were involved in any of the dredge's operations.

Prestea

Next stop on our gold mining tour was the mine at Prestea, which is located in the Western Region of Ghana. Mining at the Prestea deposit started in the 1870s and continued until 2002, during which time it produced approximately nine million ounces of gold, making it the second biggest mine by production in Ghana after the leading mine at Obuasi near Kumasi.

We didn't go "shafting" at Prestea. Instead, we had meetings in the company's board room. The managing director of the mine was an oboruni, a colloquial term in Ghana for "white man". This portly, white haired, and aged gentleman believed that we were from some funding agency. He pitched over and over the financial needs of the mine. They were considerable. The feeling amongst our group was that Prestea's mine had lost its glitter, but that there were considerable untapped deposits that could be profitably mined.

Obuasi

The last mine we visited was the mine at Obuasi, about sixty kilometres south of Kumasi, the "garden city". Kumasi is the second largest city in Ghana. It is commonly seen as the home of the Ashanti ("Asante") tribe. The mine at Obuasi is the largest mine in Ghana and one of the largest gold mines in the world. It has been producing gold for hundreds of years, although its corporate structure began only in 1870.

We were hosted at the mine's guest house where we spent the night and dined, with food and drink to excess. The next dizzy morning, we were taken by means of the main shaft to the area of underground mining operations. Once in the cage at Obuasi, we knew we were working with a different class of mine. The hoist and cage were well maintained, and the swinging adventure in the Tarkwa shaft was not repeated on this trip to the depths of the earth.

Underground, the operations were better organized and cleaner than at Tarkwa. The management team we met at Obuasi was confident and assured. They were the number one mine in Ghana and proud to show us why. They too were looking for financing for the future developments they wanted to undertake.

Before we went into the shaft, we were taken to their above ground offices to view some of the spectacular gold-bearing rocks which they had mined over the years. There was a collection of about a dozen rocks, each covered with feathery pieces of pure gold, looking like gold tin foil, which were multi-layered on each of the rocks we admired. None of these had been used to make gold bars; these were evidence of how rich the gold deposit was at Obuasi. These rocks were "brought out" to show to future investors or purchasers that one could literally peal the gold off the rocks at Obuasi. This image has been with me since that day in 1980.

We also met two outstanding Ghanaians involved with the Ashanti Gold company at Obuasi. First was the Deputy Managing Director, Lloyd. A geologist by training, he become the first senior Ghanaian in the management of the company. As impressive was the Chief Technical Officer, Sam. Who could have read his tea leaves at that time? Sam went on to become CEO of the company and CEO of the company after the merger with AngloGold of South Africa. I was fortunate to have a taste of the future of Ghana at that time.

Visit to Kumasi

We returned to Accra by driving north to Kumasi, to see Ghana's second largest city, and then turned southeast for the two hundred fifty kilometre trip to Accra. From my days in Malawi, I recalled that Dr. Banda, who had been practicing medicine on Harley Street in London, first returned to Africa by way of Ghana. He set up a surgery in Kumasi where he practiced medicine from 1953 to 1958, when he heeded the pleas of many of the younger Nyasaland Congress Party leaders for him to return to Malawi to lead their party in their quest for Independence. Dr. Banda's move to Ghana was rumoured to have been necessary because a certain nurse in his UK surgery got pregnant. A child was born, and many have said that this was Dr. Banda's only living child. He denied this vehemently whenever asked, for his entire life.

As we entered the city centre of Kumasi, I encouraged Ben to help me find Dr. Banda's surgery, even though he had left Ghana twenty-two years earlier. We stopped the car near a taxi rank, and Ben asked if anyone knew where Dr. Banda's surgery was located. Lo and behold, one driver said he knew exactly where it was. He led us there, barely a ten-minute drive. Of course, I got out and went into the one-story building, which was a series of six rooms somehow connected together like Topsy. The rooms were unkempt, loaded with files and other odds and ends; all rooms were in need of both paint and furniture.

The people there said that this was for sure Dr. Banda's surgery. One or two of the older people there said they had come to the surgery back in the day to see Dr. Banda; and they offered to show me all the rooms. What a trip back in time that was! I imagined the diminutive Dr. Banda, wearing a three-piece suit, ambling through these rooms every day, dispensing medical advice and medicine to the needy of Kumasi. This was the highlight of my visit to Ghana, a trip back in time to the holiest of holies for a Malawian, the medical practice of the future President.

The drive back to Accra was a long one, well over five hours, over roads filled with potholes. Traffic at times was heavy, especially when a lorry or two crowded the otherwise open road. The crops seen from the car were healthy and green, confirming the rumour that if one throws a seed in the air in Ghana, it will sprout as soon as it hits the ground.

Accra was a welcome sight as we returned to our rooms at the Continental Hotel. We met the next morning to organize the report we were expected to write, to shop in the market one last time and to say goodbyes to Ben and our other new friends. I was not sure exactly why I was on the mission with Peter, as I was never asked to provide any legal advisory work during the mission. Apparently, that was to become to centrepiece of my next visit to Accra.

1981

After the mission to Ghana with Peter in 1980, I thought my work for the GPC and the mining sector of Ghana had finished. For most of 1980, there was little follow up from our mission. We filed our report, which experienced the same fate of other aid reports which are prepared on Africa. Usually sleeping on the floor of one ministry and/or another. All was quiet for the rest of the year, as I continued my business activities in Nairobi.

Then in the spring of 1981, I was asked by the UNDP to return to Ghana to assist in writing a new mining law. This was a surprise to me, as I had little experience in the drafting of mining laws. My only experience had been in Zambia while working at Citibank. Nevertheless, I was soon to return to Ghana for some legal drafting. I had a feeling that Peter's hand was in this somehow. But the upcoming trip was to be a solo effort by myself.

Search for a Hotel Room

This time, my visit was more organized (or so I thought). The UNDP office in Accra was in touch with me, by telex (what else could one use at that time?), to arrange my visa and my work schedule. With many happy thoughts of the previous year's visit to Ghana, I flew off to Accra from Nairobi. I arrived about six o'clock in the evening, and after clearing Immigration, I was met by two UNDP representatives, Cecilia and Gerald. I had received my visa while in Nairobi, so I didn't have to go to the side room where I'd previously deposited a five-dollar bill into an open, cluttered drawer. Of the two young people who met me, Gerald was the driver and Cecilia was the administrator who would find me a hotel. Little did I know what the remainder of that night would be like.

For reasons I didn't understand, UNDP had not yet booked a hotel room for me. Cecilia said it should be easy to find one as there were many hotels in Accra.

First, we went to the Continental Hotel, where Peter and I had stayed during the previous year's visit. Despite every plea I made, the hotel remained fully booked. There was some hope, however. I could stay there the rest of my mission. I only had to find a hotel room elsewhere for one night. Since it was getting late, the three of us had a quick dinner at the Continental Hotel and then returned to our hotel seeking pilgrimage.

I cannot remember the names of all the hotels we went to in Accra during the next four hours. Every single one was fully booked. Not one empty room anywhere. I was getting desperate, although Gerald and Cecelia didn't seem to have a worry in the world. They were confident I would find a room for one night. They had their own homes to return to, so not much pressure there.

As we travelled by car around the capital city of Ghana, Gerald and Cecilia spoke to each other in that fast, slurred Ghanaian speech format which was new to my ear. Over and over I had to ask them to repeat what they said. I was listening to English in an English-speaking country and had no idea what my two new friends were talking about. This added to my frustration of not being able to find a hotel room.

Near midnight, we ended up at what seemed to be the last hotel in Accra: the Frimaj Palace Hotel. This was a three-story building, shaped like a rectangular box, sited on one of the busiest streets in Accra, day or night. When I approached the reception desk, I was not hopeful. But lo and behold, there was one room remaining – the biggest (and only) suite in the hotel. Its cost: three hundred Ghanaian cedis. At the official rate of one US dollar to one Ghanaian cedi, that would cost me three hundred US dollars. The most expensive hotel room I had ever stayed in. When I describe what the hotel room was like, then one might question why I paid even one Ghanaian cedi for the room.

Fortunately the next day, before checking out, I went to the UNDP office and met with a senior official of UNDP, an American named Larry. He was kind enough to convert my US dollars at the black market rate of one US dollar to twenty Ghanaian cedis. This means I eventually paid fifteen US dollars for the hotel room, still well above its market value. Why?

First of all, the hotel was on a busy street. All night, people walked and talked on the street, cars whizzed by, horns blasted endlessly (the favourite way of raising your voice as a driver in Ghana) – a cacophony for my sleeping pleasure. I would have closed the windows except that the temperature outside was over ninety degrees and the humidity even higher. With no air conditioning at the Frimaj Palace Hotel, I had to keep the windows open all night to avoid suffocation by introducing a small breeze through the windows. Still, all of this would have been tolerable. There was one thing that wasn't tolerable.

When I went to use the bathroom, I made a horrific discovery. There were cockroaches in the bathroom. And when I looked, also in the bedroom. And in the closet. Everywhere!! These were not normal sized cockroaches. No. These were Ghanaian monsters, as long as five inches each. Frightening monsters. In their dozens. I spent the next hour or more trying to de-cockroach the room. Hitting them, catching them in toilet paper, hammering them with shoes and other hard objects. Each destroyed cockroach went to heaven through the toilet. I'd fill it up, flush. Kill, fill, flush. Repeat. Again and again. When I could find no more cockroaches, I was exhausted. I had flown from Nairobi that day, spent hours looking for a hotel and now, when finally in a hotel room, I had a night of giant cockroach encounters in front of me.

I probably slept less than two hours that night. Exhausted from the flight and the endless cockroach kills, I was barely awake the next morning. And in my mind, this room was going to cost me three hundred dollars. I didn't know Larry would solve my liquidity problems the next morning so I fretted about everything.

Not a Mining Law; an Investment Promotion Law

After paying the bill for my sleepless night at the Frimaj Palace Hotel, and thankfully departing that hotel forever, I returned to Larry's office at UNDP. I was excited to hear about what my assignment was to be, expecting nervously that I would be working on a draft mining law for one of the major mining countries in Africa. That was not to be. Larry told me to forget about drafting a mining law. At the urgent request of the Government, instead I was asked to assist the Government in drafting an investment promotion law. A Government team had prepared an initial draft which they wanted me to review to ensure that it met international standards. I had never worked on an investment promotion law before; I said nothing to Larry. Because of the urgency to enact this law, they asked if I could review the draft law over the weekend and prepare a revised draft by Monday morning. Monday morning? It was Friday afternoon! Of course, I said I would do it, without thinking of the consequences. I spent twelve or more hours on each of the following days, Saturday and Sunday, cooped up in my hotel room (at least it was at the Continental Hotel – at the Frimaj Palace I would have succumbed to the cockroach onslaught). No tours, no beach, no rest. Just a fun-filled weekend in my hotel room in Accra, typing away (on a typewriter, not a computer) as I revised the draft investment promotion law. Not only was I asked to make changes; I had to annotate the changes. Endless hours in a dark hotel room in one of the most exciting cities in Africa; just me and my typewriter. Another mind-numbing event in the exciting life of an international lawyer.

I can't remember if Larry or the Government of Ghana cared much about my hard-working weekend. They had my revised and annotated draft; that's all that mattered.

Larry then told me that the next item on my agenda was to attend a meeting of the Parliamentary Sub-Committee on Investment, so that I could answer questions about my revised draft law and the proposed changes I had made. I had never been before any parliamentary or congressional committee anywhere. It was intimidating.

The day of the hearing loomed near. There was no way to prepare myself for the testimony I was to give. Merely to know my revised draft of the law backwards and forwards. I was led into the Parliament Building, in a windowless meeting room where the Sub-Committee always held its hearings. The room had a small balcony where members of the public could attend and listen to the hearings. When I looked up into the public gallery, I noticed that it was filled with young people, noisily holding placards and making it difficult to hear the questions from the Sub-Committee members. I had prepared an introductory statement, which I gave nervously. Then the questions started to flow.

It didn't take long for the public gallery to shout and scream about the loss of Ghana's National Patrimony if the new law was enacted. Foreign investors would take the profits of Ghana's resources for themselves. Most of the members in the public gallery were university students and any sort of investment promotion law would mean that Ghanaians would have to share their natural and other resources with foreign investors. It was not of importance to these university students that Ghana would gain capital, technology, jobs, training and marketing assistance from foreign investors. Each project would develop national assets of Ghana and the profits would be shared between foreign and local investors. The students in the gallery howled at any suggestion I made that Ghana's mines, agriculture and industrial outputs would be in any way owned or controlled by foreigners. At times, the gallery shouted so loudly, I couldn't be heard. The Sub-Committee members must have seen similar demonstrations in the past; they were calm in the face of the mockery and noise from the gallery. This was a major learning experience for me.

The rest is history. Notwithstanding the objections of the university students, Ghana enacted its first Investment Law in 1981, based on the advice I had given on the draft law. Over the next thirty-seven years, I returned to Ghana three more times to assist in revising the then current investment promotion law or introducing a new law. This was done in 1993, 2008 and 2018. For these three missions, I was a consultant with either the Foreign Investment Advisory Service (FIAS) of the World Bank or as a consultant to either IFC or the World Bank.

I cut my investment law advisory teeth in Ghana in 1981 which gave me credibility for future work with FIAS, IFC and the World Bank in thirty more countries over the next almost four decades. My cooped-up weekend in Accra so many years before proved to be a godsend and helped me in future years to make friends in each of these thirty new countries.

I also wrote to the Ghana Tourist Board and complained about my one-night stand at the Frimaj Palace Hotel. After a couple months, I received a letter from the Board stating how sorry they were about my stay in Ghana. They promised to take appropriate action against the Frimaj Palace Hotel. I doubt that the Board did anything with the hotel. When last in Ghana I tried to find the Frimaj Palace Hotel and was not able to locate this paragon of hospitality. The market dealt with the hotel and consigned it to where it belonged.

Completed: December 10, 2020

LEGAL EAGLES

Setting up a Law Office in a Foreign Country

Zdravstvyite. Hello. Po-Russkiy. From the moment I landed in Moscow on April 17, 1994 to start my new job as head of the office a large American law firm, I kept trying to say: zdravstvyite. Over and over. By January 1995, I finally had completed the challenge. Zdravstvyite. A perfect introduction to the Russian language.

Through a series of circumstances that no one could have ever imagined, I had travelled from my first trip to Africa in December 1966, to my move to Nairobi in October 1975, my move back to Washington, DC in August 1983, my first visit to Moscow in September 1991, and finally my arrival that April 17th day of 1994 to begin managing the new Moscow office of Akin Gump Strauss Hauer and Feld, LLP, more commonly known as Akin Gump. It was a journey of unimaginable twists and turns, including moments of tension, doubt, disappointment, surprise, awe and pleasure. That is the journey we shall embark upon together, culminating in the establishment of a law office in Moscow, Russia for one of America's largest international law firms.

Overseas with Peace Corps

This journey began with small steps long ago when I arrived in Malawi on January 1, 1967 to serve for two years as a Peace Corps Volunteer, teaching high school

English at HHI Secondary School in Blantyre. The decision to apply to the Peace Corps was the single most important decision of my life. The pushing of the rock off the top of the hill. I had no idea where the rock would end up, but the fact that it started moving led me on an international adventure which was outside the ken of a suburban Chicago boy.

How quickly my first five years in Malawi passed. Teaching English, organizing sports locally and nationally, training the No. 1 tennis player in the country, and then serving as the international legal advisor to the Malawi Government ministry responsible for external affairs. I also met and married my wife and we began our family during this formative time. This springboard catapulted me into the World Bank legal department in January 1972, three months after we returned from overseas. I also served as the third Chairman of the World Bank Staff Association during my tenure at the Bank. Soon after, I arrived in Nairobi, Kenya as a neophyte banker for First National City Bank of New York in October 1975. Both my international career and family continued to grow.

Kenya with Citibank

In 1976, my employer became known as Citibank. After an exciting two years of managing Citibank's business in Malawi, Tanzania and Zambia (with some side jaunts to Madagascar), my tenure in Nairobi was threatened the following year when Bob wanted to send me to Nigeria to run Citibank's future operations there. He was rewarding me for a job well done in Nairobi. For a series of reasons, I never made it to Nigeria in the employ of Citibank. Instead, I met the law firm of Duncan, Allen and Mitchell (DAM) during a holiday visit to Washington, D.C. They already had offices in Kinshasa, Zaire and Abidjan, Ivory Coast. The "belt and road" office that was missing, mimicking China's "belt and road initiative", was in Nairobi, Kenya. After my meeting, they decided to open an office there in January 1978, with Pat Mitchell as the managing partner and myself as the only associate.

After founding the firm in 1970 with Emerson and Don, Pat originally opened the first African office of DAM in Kinshasa in 1972 and had a long and successful career in that difficult market. By 1978 he and his family were exhausted by the uncertainties of living in Kinshasa. This was one reason he wanted to move his family to a safer and more stable country. He had already gone through the throes of opening a law office in one African country. How could I not learn from him?

DAM Office in Nairobi, Kenya

I joined DAM in late January 1978. Our first project was to find office space. Fortunately, Kenya Commercial Bank (KCB) was opening its new headquarters building in early 1978. There were a few floors of this eight-story building that were designed and designated for commercial lessees like DAM. We ended up on the sixth floor. When I say "ended up", I mean we agreed to lease an area of two thousand square feet which was completely open when we first walked through it. No walls or doors, no phone, and no computers or wifi, neither of which existed at that time. Just an open area with windows. An interior designer's dream.

The first objective in the office was to make a floor plan. We divided the office space into four offices, a reception area, a conference room and a library. Toilets were outside the office at the end of the floor and shared by all on the floor. KCB required that we use their chosen company for the construction of the internal walls and another company for the electrical and telephone systems. The colour scheme was also decided by KCB although we could decorate the walls with paintings, photographs and other objects d'art.

Along with the establishment of the office, we had to establish ourselves. I had a work permit from my Citibank days, which was easy to transfer, but Pat had to start from scratch. Getting a work permit was not easy, but still not as hard as it is now. Eventually we each paid KSh2,000 ($280) for a two-year work permit. As consultants; no mention was made of our legal skills or intentions. We set up bank accounts with Citibank, because of my recent employment there. I was already a member of Parklands Club for tennis and other social activities. Pat decided to make his home his sports and social centre.

As far as the licensing requirements for practicing law in Kenya were concerned, there were requirements -- and we did not qualify. An American legal education was not considered adequate for the practice of law in Kenya. We therefore established Duncan Allen and Mitchell Limited, a business consulting company with some pretty good ideas about the legal aspects of doing business in a country like Kenya. This did not go down well with some of the local lawyers in Kenya.

After a year, Pat and I were able to arrange a meeting with Amos, the Kenyan President of the Law Society of Kenya (LSK), and Paul, a Kenyan member of the Council of the LSK who was not pleased with our efforts to establish a presence in Kenya. We had hoped that by meeting Amos and Paul, who represented the legal supervisory authorities, we would find a way to accommodate our desire to practice law in Kenya. The meeting was held in a quiet and windowless room. Amos was friendly and we bantered with him for about thirty minutes before Paul even said one word. When Paul opened his mouth, he said forcibly that if he had this way, we would be charged with practicing law illegally, which might have led to imprisonment. He wanted us out of Kenya quickly since we were not authorized to practice law. Pat and I were not surprised that we were not welcome; we were surprised with the aggressiveness and demeanour shown by Paul.

This was Paul's nature. Grab the situation with his hands, push aggressively and look mean and angry while doing this. He succeeded. However, within three years, the pendulum swung the other way. Paul was hounded by several politicians around President Moi, who succeeded President Kenyatta in August 1978. In 1982, Paul's life was at risk. He was active politically and his methods were not appreciated. Without any thought of the incongruity of his position, Paul met the US Ambassador and begged to be given a visa to go to the US so that he could leave Kenya, save his life and work in the United States. The fact that he had tried to kick two US citizens out of Kenya in 1979 was forgotten. Fortunately, the US Ambassador had not forgotten how Paul treated Pat and me. Paul stayed in Kenya without being issued a US visa.

Most lawyers and others in Nairobi were friendly to us, notwithstanding that we were on the fringe of the legal community. And many were happy to retain our services as "business" consultants (with very good legal skills). Paul was one of the few Kenyan lawyers who was hell bent on removing us from Kenya. Another "friend" of ours was John, the managing partner of an eighty-year-old white law firm, one of the two large law firms in Kenya. John never met us. But he went out of his way to blackball my membership application to the Muthaiga Club, which I had wanted to join so that I could play tennis with some friends of mine. The purpose of his blackball? To get even with us for taking away some clients of his law firm. In the end, John's blackball was effective. I never was able to become a member of the

Muthaiga Club. On the other hand, DAM continued to exist and prosper.

Back to 1978. We now had an office. We had two lawyers, Pat and me. Next we needed an employee in the office to do things other than provide business (and legal) services. Our first recruit was Jean, who answered phones, did secretarial work and supported our various business activities. Jean was a Ugandan, short and smart, and well connected. Although the East African Community had collapsed in 1977, citizens of each of the three member countries, Kenya, Tanzania and Uganda, were still able to work in the other two countries as well.

Fortunately, I didn't have to find a place to live in Nairobi, as I kept the house in Kilileshwa which my family and I had occupied when I was working for Citibank. Pat found a home in Karen, a suburb south of the city. It had lots of land and a tennis court. My infamous match with Emerson, the senior founding partner of DAM, took place on that court. I was not proud of the score; Pat was furious that I didn't lose more than one point, and that a double fault.

We decided to keep office expenses lower by not buying an office car. Pat and I each had our own cars. We had a messenger in the office to move documents around the city centre. We did not have computers. We did not have cell phones. We did not have facsimiles. None of these were invented and available at that time. We only had phones and telex. Compared to today, it was amazing that we could get any work done.

In our first year in Kenya, we represented the Mt Kenya Safari Club (the managing director Ed became close friends of both of us), the Schaffer Sugar Company of Baton Rouge, La., (Ned, their CFO, had worked with our partner Hunt in Abidjan), and a couple families of Indian origin who were trying to raise monies for their businesses. Because of my warm connections with the Citibank office, we were retained to represent a couple Citibank-led, offshore lending syndicates with transactions in Malawi and Zambia.

The office began reasonably well, but the costs of operating in Kenya were considerable. We did not have a client base sufficient to sustain this model forever. By 1981, we knew that we needed to do something else. Pat had met Salim, a local solo practitioner whom he thought would make a strong addition to our team. He was right. In January 1982, we brought Salim on board and changed the name of the firm to Duncan, Allen, Mitchell and Dhanji (DAMD). We had determined through research that with Salim's name in the firm, we could overtly practice law, using Salim's name as part of the firm name. At least Salim could. Pat and I remained in the background, doing research, writing, attending meetings with clients who knew our situation, but never signing any documents and never appearing in court.

Change of Direction in 1982

With Salim's presence in the firm, within three months, we were retained by Citibank, First National Bank of Chicago, Commercial Bank of Africa (Bank of America) and ALICO, the American Life Insurance Company. Part of our growth was due to the friendships and relationships which Pat and I had developed from 1978. But also, Salim proved to be a superb learner and an even better lawyer. His small, litigation-based practice grew into the largest banking practice in Kenya.

One other step we took helped us to achieve this rapid growth. After reviewing the details of the Law Society of Kenya's rules on scale fees, we realized that lawyers were not required to charge scale fees, the high percentage fees that the white law firms had engineered when setting up the legal system. For most of the high level corporate and commercial work, which had been the bread and butter of the white law firms, they had charged scale fees, a percentage of the deal, rather than fees based on time expended on a matter. The result was the banks and insurance companies were charged extraordinarily high fees for drafting documents that became easier and easier to prepare as the computer revolution started and grew. These high costs were passed directly on to their borrowers, and eventually the consumers in Kenya.

We determined that scale fees were only advised by the LSK, not required. DAMD proposed to its growing client list to charge fees based on our time expended, not on an unrelated scale fee. This brought down dramatically the costs of the preparation and negotiation of most legal documents for the banking and insurance sectors. We obviously were on to something as within six months of establishing new fee charges for our clients, all the major law firms in Kenya were doing the same thing. The cost of legal services took a tumble in Kenya. But then, where there is good, always something not so good arises.

The bank officers at some of the banks which were our clients found a way to abuse our new fee practice. Those bank officers who had the responsibility for selecting law firms to draft their loan and security documents seized the moment. Instead of selecting law firms who all charged the same scale fees, the bank officers could select law firms with different fee levels for the same work. Even more relevant, their decisions on which law firm to choose were not subject to review. So, their decisions were final. This brought a new practice into being. Law firms were asked by bank officers to quote their new, non-scale fee levels, but also, quietly, were asked to make a not so "token" payment to the bank officer whose decision it was to retain the law firm. DAMD never made such payments. By reducing the costs of drafting legal instruments for borrowers and consumers, we had designed a system that contributed to corruption in the Kenyan banking community. We did not see that one coming.

Once our practice had settled down with Salim in the lead, we needed to enlarge the DAMD staff to handle the increased workload. In October 1982, we hired Murugi, our first local associate. She was bright, energetic and fit well into our growing law practice. Mina had replaced Jean as secretary for Pat and me. We hired Josephine as Salim's secretary, John as court clerk and Anset as messenger. Anset proved to be a project, as his attention wavered from time to time, and his lackadaisical demeanour proved to be a distraction. In the end, Anset used his initial time in DAMD to build a career as court clerk for other law firms. A real success story.

From our initial steps into Kenya in 1978, we had built a formidable law practice, with capable colleagues and a genial office atmosphere. This was to become the template for my next experience in opening a law office in another foreign country, the time in Moscow, Russia.

Return to DAM's Washington, D.C. office in 1983

With pressure from my wife to have our growing family of four daughters return to the US, we left Kenya in August 1983. When I arrived at the DAM Washington DC office, the next month I was made the Managing Partner of the firm. The bulk of my practice remained focused on Africa, to which I travelled frequently, while also taking over the management of the firm and its four offices, three of which were in Africa. This situation lasted until May 1988, when Pat, Rick (an associate in our Zaire office), and I left DAM to set up a new law firm, MFG. We opened a new office in Washington, D.C., thanks in large part to the support of my close friend Roger, a fraternity brother of mine in AEPi, and also a graduate of the University of Wisconsin. He allowed us to sublet space in his law firm's office, which gave us support that we would have otherwise had to develop on our own.

The MFG experiment lasted until April 1991. By that time, we had offices in Washington, DC, Kinshasa, Zaire, Brussels, Belgium (where Rick spent most of this time), and Addis Ababa, Ethiopia where I engineered setting up a branch of our law firm with Teshome, a dear and talented Ethiopian friend of mine. A bit too extended for a three partner law firm. Too many offices, too few clients, too little cash flow – which led to Pat announcing at the end of March 1991 that he was leaving the partnership to live in Johannesburg.

Fortunately, I had made friends with an Irish lawyer at Akin Gump. As MFG fell apart, Rick in Brussels and I in Washington approached Akin Gump and were both hired. I joined the International Section of Akin Gump. It was my first experience working in a large, private law firm, which had at that time four hundred fifty lawyers. At least I had joined a law firm for which an office was not needed to be established. This luxury only lasted three years.

Akin Gump Office in Moscow, Russia

For reasons not relevant here, I had the largest Russian client in Akin Gump in 1993. To service this client, I visited Moscow six times in 1993. Some of my visits were with Jay, the experienced litigation partner who led the Russian international arbitration matter I had brought into the firm in November 1992. We were dining in 1993 late one June night at a new restaurant near Taganskaya Metro Station. When dessert and coffee appeared, Jay gave me a "head's up". He asked if I would like to live in Moscow. When I queried his query, he eventually "fessed" up, on a most confidential basis, that the Managing Partner of the firm, Bruce, was thinking of asking me to head up Akin Gump's possible new office in Moscow in 1994. Our senior partner, Bob Strauss, had been the US Ambassador to the Soviet Union from August 1991 until he left as US Ambassador to the Russian Federation in November 1992. Because of US Government ethics rules, Bob's firm could not enter the Russian market until one year after he left his position. That date was approaching.

I remember my first reaction – to myself. Of course, I would do it. Why not? I was excited as this meant that Bob would have known of my work and would have approved me as the head of the new office. We would work together closely in the planning, implementation and management of the new Moscow office. But at that dinner, I was circumspect with Jay, since I had not discussed this with my family. I said I would consider it.

Fast forward to a late October night in 1993 at the Metropol Hotel in the centre of Moscow. Or should I say early morning. Jay, Bruce and I were drinking in the bar at about 1 am. It had been, as always, a long day and we were all exhausted. The bar was loud and busy, as it was in all Moscow hotels at this time of the evening. Out of the blue, Bruce began to talk to me about the firm, its plans, and the successes which we hoped to achieve by enlarging our practice in Russia. To do this, he said, would require the firm to open an office in Moscow. He said the office would have to be led by someone in whom the firm had confidence, someone who would succeed in getting the office up and running. He poured me another drink (it was endless in those days), looked me in the eye and said, "Jim, we want you to be that person. Are you willing to come to Moscow and open the Akin Gump office?"

Notwithstanding Jay's warning of five months before, I was lost for words. I knew I wanted to accept but told Bruce that I needed to consult with my wife and children first. I promised to do this within ten days of returning home.

In the summer of 1993, my wife and I had decided to open a coffee shop in Leesburg, Virginia in November 1993. She wanted to work since the kids were growing and leaving the home nest one by one. We had just rented a store space, bought equipment, signed up suppliers and within three weeks of my return from Moscow, Coffee 'N More was to be born. Because of her commitment to her new enterprise, my wife said I should take the offer and go to Moscow. She and the kids would not come with me. Instead, I arranged with the firm that I would visit my home in Virginia at least once every three months, for about ten days each time.

Preparations for Moscow in Washington, DC

The clock started ticking. We needed a plan and a time frame. The firm gave me both. I had started working with Natalia, a young, Russian associate as early as February 1993. She had a doctorate in law from a Russian university and had received her LLM from the University of Illinois in 1992. Upon graduation she was hired by a Texas-based firm; nine months later she joined Akin Gump's Washington DC office. That year Natalia became my "go-to" lawyer on Russian law, a situation that remains the same today. Although I was not made aware of it at the time, the firm intended that Natalia would return to Moscow to practice law when Akin Gump opened its office in 1994. We were scheduled to be colleagues in Akin Gump's newest office.

We needed legs on the ground in Moscow, instead of frequent trips in and out of the country, to develop and control the establishment of the office. Bob had employed a young American, John, to be his driver in Moscow during his tenure as Ambassador. John had been studying in Moscow at that time, and readily jumped on the bandwagon to work with Bob. As I had done. John then returned to the US after Bob left his ambassadorial post and was working in Washington DC when he got a call from Bob. I think it took one nanosecond for John to agree to return to Moscow as office manager of the soon-to-be new Akin Gump office.

John and I got along from the start. We met in December 1993 for the first time, just before the holiday season. His engaging smile was present from day one. He was young, eager, yet wise in the ways of life in Moscow. John made easy many of the difficult aspects of starting a new law firm in a foreign city. He was fluent in Russian, something I would never achieve in my lifetime. And he loved living in Moscow. The opportunity to return to Moscow and work with a large American law firm gave John purpose which he attacked with considerable energy.

After our first meeting, we met and made a detailed plan for things John would do before Natalia and I arrived. After the plan was approved by Bruce, John moved to Moscow in January 1994. We now had legs on the ground. At the same time, I was visiting Kiev to finalize Akin Gump's recent big win: a World Bank-funded contract with the Government of Ukraine to revise its upstream oil and gas legislation. I intended to visit Moscow after Kiev, but on the next to last day, I was shocked when informed by my family that my older brother, Bob, had passed away. I immediately flew back to the US the next day, on the newly established yellow and blue wings of Air Ukraine. I was not able to return to Moscow until mid-February to meet John and discuss the various options we had for office space, apartment space, cars, drivers, telecommunications, banking, and the endless matters that one must deal with before an office can "go live".

The big issue when opening a law firm is the amount and cost of office space. The firm agreed that we should lease about 2,000 square feet of space in an old building being refurbished by a Canadian/Russian joint venture. This was the style of the day, joint ventures between foreign and local construction firms. The three-story building, with its own parking lot in the back, was located on Bolshoi Sukharevsky pereulok (per.). We signed the lease agreement for the office space in March, but refurbishment would not be concluded until October 1994. What to do in the meantime as we wanted to open the office as soon as possible? Again, John found the perfect option: leasing a room for six months in the Americom Business Centre, which was attached to the Radisson-Slavjanskaya Hotel complex near Kievskaya Metro Station. We signed the lease for the room in March 1994 and we were ready to open our law factory, as the Russians used to call law firms.

Another issue that applied in other countries but not in Russia at this time was the licensing of lawyers. We were the 28th foreign law firm to open in Moscow, so we had the benefit of their experiences in dealing with the licensing requirements. In fact, there were none since we did not intend to practice before the courts in Russia.

Akin Gump's Moscow Office Opens in 1994

Akin Gump officially opened its Russian door (we only had one in that small room) on April 18, 1994. That was my first day in the office, after arriving late afternoon the day before. Natalia had been in Moscow since March, working with John on getting the room in the Americom Business Centre up and running. That April day is another milestone in the history of Akin Gump. It was the first meeting in Moscow with what would become the firm's largest Russian client, LUKOIL, at that time the largest oil and gas company in Russia. There are not enough bytes left in this story to write the long history of that mutually beneficial relationship, merely to mention its beginning. Nor is there room to describe all the characters and situations we found ourselves in during and after that six months at the Americom Centre. For example, two and a half years later, one potential American client who was part owner of the Americom Centre was gunned down in a hail of eleven bullets as he entered the Kievskaya Metro Station. This is not the only story which would shock and stun our small team.

During the six months we were developing our client base from the Americom Centre room, we continually visited the new office at Bolshoi Sukharevsky per. to meet with the contractors and other suppliers that would eventually complete the building in time for our scheduled October opening. Endless numbers of decisions relating to the office, furniture, colours, technology, staff, letterhead had to be made. Without John, this never would have happened on time.

In our new offices, we were located in two wings on the first floor (second floor in US terms), split by the staircase which went up through the middle of the building and which served on the ground floor as a smoking place (место курения). Already Moscow was showing signs of health issues in the workplace. On the ground floor below us were a small law firm called Rothstein & Shaw, and a German screw company called Würth. Above us were the offices of the English law firm, Norton Rose.

As head of the office, I had my own room at the front of the building with a window that overlooked the street and a small park with an ever-present, all year kvass kiosk. The others, lawyers and support staff, shared open space desks. We also had a conference room and a kitchen to feed lunch every day to the hungry workers (including ourselves) pursuant to existing Russian legislation. We hired Maya as cook and cleaner as soon as we moved into the new office.

The telecommunications facilities were those of the day, nothing very sophisticated. During the first week we were in the new office, Bob was in Moscow. He came by the office, bursting with pride over the new Akin Gump flag now planted where he had his greatest success as a diplomat. In honour of his visit, we asked Bob to make the first telephone call to our Washington, DC office.

I'll never forgot the smile on his face as he called Bruce to confirm that Akin Gump's new office in Moscow was up and running.

The only computer connection we had to the outside world was through my small laptop and printer. With the network unstable and slow, it would often take as long as five minutes to download one page of a document. Given the size of legal documents for our client base, this meant I spent an extraordinary amount of time trying to connect with the Washington, DC office and download documents. When viewed from the technology of today, we were in dinosaur times, not much further than when I was assisting the Malawi Government as a Treaties Officer in 1969. Nevertheless, we made do and somehow accomplished extraordinary results from a technology base that could not support the speed and breadth of our clients' needs.

Looking back to that April day in 1994, when the Moscow office of Akin Gump began with Natalia, John and me, two lawyers and one office manager, one could not see the future. We were all crowded into a two hundred square foot room. A stark beginning to what would become arguably Akin Gump's most successful office over the next more than thirty years. The lessons of Kenya and other international offices I had been associated with came to roost. We planted the Akin Gump flag, which flew strongly in the winds of Russia. Bob was proud of what he and the firm had wrought and remained so for the rest of his life. For me, it was the culmination of my adventures in establishing legal practices in the far reaches of the world.

Completed: March 18, 2021

IN THE SHADOW OF THE HIMALAYAS

Namaste. Kathmandu. The capital of Nepal. An exotic name for a mysterious place. Kathmandu. The name means "wooden pavilion" and recalls a building which existed in the main square of this city many centuries ago. Kathmandu. A name with a difference. It evokes the East, the mystery, the unknown, the spiritual lives and peoples of this far away and ancient mountain kingdom.

Annapurna: mountain, region and hotel. How did Annapurna (and Kathmandu) come into my life? It might seem strange that a fifty-year Africa hand with also more than thirty years of living and work experience in the former Soviet Union would have any connection with the Kingdom of Nepal--or should I say the Federal Democratic Republic of Nepal. Doesn't roll off the tongue, does it?

Return to US from Malawi

My nearest potential encounter with Nepal in earlier years was in 1971. My wife and I took an around-the-world trip to the East after leaving Malawi. We spent more than two weeks in India and Kashmir on our way back to the United States. Although we never thought about visiting Nepal on that trip, within two years I would be the World Bank lawyer responsible for all Bank projects in Nepal.

Upon our arrival in Los Angeles in August 1971, I began to interview for jobs. We travelled through Los Angeles, San Francisco, Phoenix, Chicago and New York, as I interviewed in each city for jobs in such sectors as law, international banking, commercial banking and the airline industry. Five cities, no job offers. Even Pan American Airlines in New York City did not feel that my international background was appropriate for their business. That was fortunate, given the eventual demise of iconic airline.

Our last stop was in Washington, D.C. where we arrived on October 3rd and decided to stay until I had a job offer. Our decision to stay in Washington, D.C. was based mainly on the fact that my wife was pregnant; our first child was due in January 1972. This was a risky strategy as the Nixon Administration's "wage-price" freeze for the U.S. Government was introduced in August 1971. I was trying to find a job in Washington D.C. during a U.S. Government hiring freeze. Great timing!

Fortunately, we were able to stay with Jerry and Francie in their Georgetown townhouse while I looked for a job. Jerry became the Third Secretary with the US Embassy in Blantyre soon after I arrived in January 1967 to serve as a Peace Corps Volunteer. He and Francie had previously served in Kabul. Jerry later was my best man at our wedding in September 1969. We stayed on the top floor of their four-story townhouse, making it harder and harder for my wife to come downstairs each day. I started bringing her breakfast in bed every day before I headed out by foot and bus on my job search. For their most generous hospitality I paid Jerry and Francie $15 a week for room and board, which was all I could afford.

Over the next three months, I had over fifty job interviews, with private law firms, consulting firms, returned Peace Corps NGOs, U. S. Government agencies, and Congressional offices. I met some amazing people, including Senator Eagleton who offered me the job of managing D.C. Stadium because of my sports background. I was looking for a job that used my legal training so I turned down his kind job offer. Little did I know that about six months later, he would be chosen to be Senator McGovern's running mate for the 1972 presidential election. Two weeks after his selection, a news report that he had been treated for clinical depression ended his bid to be Vice President. Most of my interviews were focused on international law or business. However, not one offer came my way. While my wife was getting more and more pregnant every day, I was getting desperate.

World Bank

After almost two months of knocking on doors, shaking hands, writing letters, and making calls, fortune came my way. I had contacted my good friend Mel, who was working as the Administrative Assistant for Senator Tunney of California. Mel was a close friend of Ed, my law school roommate. They were both from Los Angeles and each had been elected the president of their successive classes at the University of California, Berkeley. Mel sent my resume to a Californian he knew named Duke who was the vice president responsible for public relations at the World Bank. Duke did what most people would in his position would do; he forwarded my resume (probably without reading it) to Ronnie, the General Counsel of the World Bank. The day before my resume landed on Ronnie's desk, an American lawyer in the Legal Department resigned from the Bank. Thus, my resume was the first American resume Ronnie saw after this resignation.

A few days later, I was called into the Bank to interview with two senior counsel in the Legal Department. Two more interviews had me in front of General Counsel Ronnie for the first time. I guess the interview went well as by the end of November, I had a job offer to join the World Bank's Legal Department. I was still twenty-nine years old, one year younger than the Bank's minimum age, as they wanted applicants to have some experience after their education was over. After the FBI completed a required report on me that each U.S. citizen who received a job offer from the Bank had to endure, my job offer was confirmed. I was requested to report to the Bank on Monday, January 3, 1972 to start my new career. I was dutifully there that Monday morning and was led through the Bank's entry process by human resources officer, Jay.

The Legal Department had no training program at that time. New lawyers like me shadowed another lawyer during negotiations. We learned by watching, questioning, and doing whatever the lawyer leading the negotiations required me to do. For one whole year, I had no countries of my own (each lawyer usually had three or four). For that first year, I was shuffled between Mexico, Swaziland, Ethiopia and negotiations with other countries. I also undertook two very special assignments for Ronnie and his number two, Lester. These assignments had nothing to do with Bank operations. One was to establish the basis for the Bank making loans for population control and one a review of the Bank's willingness to provide Bank funding to countries where expropriations had taken place since the Bank began its operations in 1944.

After a few months of this haphazard approach to training, I got frustrated. I started talking to other young lawyers in the Legal Department who had the same experience of uncertainty and helplessness that I had. By June 1972, I reached my limit. I authored a memorandum to Ronnie commenting about the lack of a training program and a career development program for lawyers in the Department. Nine other younger lawyers signed my memorandum. I was seen from that point in time as a troublemaker who was rocking the immutable system the Legal Department had followed for ages.

Staff Association

In September 1972, the Bank's management agreed to set up a Staff Association, which the staff had been requesting for the previous two years. Each department of the Bank elected a representative to the General Assembly of the Staff Association. Because of my then infamous June letter complaining about the lack of training and career development, I was overwhelmingly chosen as the Legal Department's representative to the Staff Association. Be careful what you wish for. When the selection of Executive Committee members of the Staff Association took place, I was asked to join the Executive Committee because they needed a lawyer on the management team of the Staff Association.

By September 1972, although almost the youngest Bank staff member, I was actively involved with the formation and direction of the Staff Association yet had no countries I could call my own. This changed in January 1973, when the Legal Department annually re-assigned countries to the lawyers in the Department. I finally had my first four countries for which I had primary responsibility: Guyana, Indonesia (irrigation projects only), Malawi and Nepal.

Country Lawyer for Nepal

Nepal entered my life. For the first time. Countries were allocated to lawyers by the Legal Department's senior management. In my case, I had no discussion with them on which countries I wanted, although they did know about my tie to Malawi. In those days, a lawyer could work on countries all over the world; a few years later they would be restricted to countries in specific regions.

I was excited that I finally had prime responsibility for four countries. Training was over, such as it was. Soon after these country assignments were announced, I met with the Division Chief for Nepal, Alphonse, who was from Japan. And his number two, Mohamed, an Egyptian. These were the movers and shakers of all Bank Group projects in Nepal. The sectors I remember working on from 1973 to 1975 were agriculture and irrigation, forestry, highways. telecommunications, tourism (mainly hotels), and water supply and sewerage which was to be the first project I would undertake from start to finish. The most interesting of these was tourism, as it was a new sector for the Bank, which usually left the private sector arm of the Bank, the International Finance Corporation, IFC, to develop hotels in member countries. Nepal's GDP was so low that it qualified for interest-free loans from another arm of the Bank Group, the International Development Association, IDA. As lawyers, we worked for both the Bank and IDA, the only difference in the documents being the terms of the loans or interest-free credits made by the respective institutions.

The main airport access points into Kathmandu at the time were from Bangkok, Calcutta and Delhi. The first of my four trips to Kathmandu while working for the Bank Group was in the Spring, 1973, when I flew into Nepal on a Royal Nepal Airlines Corporation (RNAC) flight from Delhi. The RNAC fleet consisted of four types of small aircraft: the Hawker-Siddeley 748, an old

DC-3 and the newly acquired De Havilland Twin Otter; its one larger aircraft was a Boeing 727 which started flying in 1972. As I recall, my first flight was on the Hawker-Siddeley 748. When the pilot made an announcement, I was surprised. A Texas accent flooded the aircraft, its mellifluous sound reminiscent of the American South. It was the first time that I understood that pilots were no different than mercenaries, but without guns. This was globalization in the strictest sense of the word. With English being the language that was required by all nations as the "language of the air", it should not have been surprising to hear English from airline pilots in the endless variety of accents which permeate the globe.

I landed safely on the short Kathmandu runway on the top of a mountain outside the city. After clearing immigration swiftly with my light blue laissez passer issued by the United Nations to all World Bank employees, I met for the first time the Bank driver in Kathmandu, Bhakta. Over the next two years, Bhakta and I became very close friends. He drove me to all meetings. We talked to each other often of our families; I even had the chance to meet his. He was loyal to the Bank Group and its mission, and very open with me in our discussions about Nepal, Nepalese traditions and religions, and life in Kathmandu during the times I was there. Whenever I saw Bhakta at the airport, I felt I had come home.

Annapurna Hotel

On that first trip, I stayed at the Annapurna Hotel, the preferred hotel for all World Bank staff. The Bank Group usually insisted that the staff stay at four-star hotels to facilitate our ability to carry out our assignments with the least amount of interference or hindrance. It was the same reason that we flew in either first class or business class at that time. The Bank Group wanted us to be able to perform from the minute we touched down, which was often required. I remember more than once being whisked from an airport to meetings with Government officials without having time to go to a hotel.

Most of my visits to Kathmandu were between one to two weeks. It was a long distance to travel for only a few days of meetings. On the first, a one-week trip, I used my time at the end of the day to walk around the city to see and feel its heartbeat. What a colourful place! Blended together were the noises of music blaring through loudspeakers, cars honking horns, people singing and talking, along with the variety of colours that one saw from religious buildings, balconies, store fronts and advertisements and the clothes and costumes traditionally worn by the Nepalese people. In addition, when one wandered the streets, the intriguing smells of unusual foods for sale wafted everywhere. It was like attending a daily carnival which was, in fact, just a day in the life of Kathmandu. But for this international visitor from Washington, D.C., it was an entry into the uniqueness of life in the East, which I would never have imagined before my walks in the late afternoons of that first visit to Kathmandu.

Among the many places to spend money in Kathmandu were jewellery stores with unusual offerings. My most interesting purchase was a gift for my wife, a handmade necklace of dozens of pieces of red garnets, green jade and pearls, all in a gold setting. I paid $80 for the necklace and earrings, $80! When I tried to value them for insurance purposes back in the U.S., the jeweller I asked for a quotation said that he could not ascribe any figure to the necklace since it was handmade, and no jeweller would have the time to carve all those stones to the quality they were carved. But in Kathmandu, the Indian jewellers, who had been there for so many years, had the time and skill to produce pieces of quality that could not be found anywhere else. This necklace was only one of the many unique pieces of jewellery I brought home from my visits to Kathmandu.

One of the main purposes of my first trip was to follow up on the Tourism Project which had been signed in 1972 before I was made the Bank lawyer responsible for projects in Nepal. There were two main aspects to this project, the renovation and expansion of the Annapurna Hotel where I was staying and the design and construction of the Yak and Yeti Hotel, using an old palace as the foundation of the new hotel which was yet to be built. The project was behind schedule, which was common in Nepal. No action was taken by the

Government of Nepal within the time frames envisioned by the credit documents signed with the Bank Group. There were some members of Government who were outstanding and who would have been successful wherever they worked, inside or outside Nepal. But these individuals were few and far between. Plus, it appeared to me that traditional Nepalese society required more of a consensus on decisions than what the Bank Group required of the Government in its documentation. Progress was slow and deliberate, frustrating for those of us anxious to see the Government move forward more quickly in meeting its development objectives.

Because I was staying at the Annapurna Hotel, I took advantage to meet with the Rana family, who owned the hotel. The family was represented by two brothers, one of whom managed the hotel on a daily basis. After the IDA Credit was signed, few of the actions required in the Credit had been taken by the Annapurna Hotel. The Credit was a year behind schedule. I remember a meeting with the Rana brothers one evening, in a special upstairs room at the Annapurna Hotel. There were three of us in the Bank Group team; the Rana brothers were two. We were offered a tasty, special dinner in the ambiance of this unique and magnificently decorated room, with musicians playing quietly out of sight and drinks poured with abandon. The room was a magnificent example of Nepalese palace ostentatiousness. The Ranas were used to having their way in Nepal, and a special dinner in a secluded room was their way to convince the Bank Group team that their approach was the right one. While the food was delicious, the ambiance seductive and the talk wide-ranging, the Ranas eventually pulled their project out of the IDA Credit as it gave too much authority and control of their hotel operations to the Bank Group. Control was not something the Ranas were used to sharing. But if you borrow from a lender as formal and strict as the Bank, something has to give.

After my first visit to Kathmandu, a horrible tragedy occurred on July 9, 1973. The Singha Durbar Palace, which contained all the major government offices including the offices of the Government's lawyers, burned down. In the destruction of the Palace, all the Government's legal documents were lost, including those for the World Bank Group. Before the fire of 1973, the Singha Durbar Palace had seven courtyards and 1700 rooms with marbled floors, painted ceilings, silver furniture and expanses of crystal lighting. From the time it was originally built in 1908, it was one of the most magnificent palaces in the world. My meetings with Government lawyers and Ministry representatives were inevitably held within this magnificent edifice. Not only were we shocked by the loss, we spent years afterwards re-creating the documents evidencing the relationship between the Kingdom and the World Bank Group.

Yak and Yeti

On my next trip in September 1973, a colleague and I went for dinner one night to the Yak and Yeti restaurant, the finest restaurant in the capital and therefore in the country. It was started by Boris Lissanevitch, a former Russian ballet dancer, Army deserter and chef, who met the King of Nepal in Calcutta in 1944 and soon after decided to make Kathmandu his home. Boris was larger than life; his full figure belied his ballet feats. Think Despicable Me. The Yak and Yeti restaurant was located in a rundown building which was the remnant of the Royal Hotel which Boris had started in the early 1950s. The Royal Hotel was in fact a refurbished palace which had been owned by the powerful Rana family, the same family that now owned and operated the Annapurna Hotel. By 1969, the Royal Hotel had become so dilapidated it was closed. The only part of the former Royal Hotel which was functioning on my visit that Fall evening was the Yak and Yeti restaurant.

To enter the restaurant, one had to walk down two long corridors, perpendicular to each other. Eventually one turned left and entered the unique and very special world of the Yak and Yeti restaurant. In the first and larger room, there were many tables. When we arrived around 7 pm, the larger room was barely occupied. We were surprised since we were told that this was "the" restaurant in Kathmandu. This room was in fact neither unique nor special. But what I had yet to see, toward the back of the room, was an entrance into the fantasy life of palatial Rana times. We walked into a semi-circular room, with a unique and large open hearth in the centre of the room. Though the evening was cold, the warmth of this room was felt as soon as one entered. The hearth was ablaze, flames sparkling and jumping, sharing its warmth and even its light not only with the six two-person tables which encircled the hearth, but also encompassing the remaining twelve tables which were placed around and against the wall of the semi-circular room. The décor of this unique room was Nepalese palatial, with furniture and wall and furniture decorations appropriate to palace life of the past. In a corner of the room, a musician was softly playing an old instrument, adding to the lure of the ambiance of the Yak and Yeti.

While each table was its own island, as if floating in the soft and changing light of the hearth's warm rays in an otherwise darkened room, the customers often talked to each other in quiet tones. It was during one of these muted conversations that a twenty-two year old woman named Kelly at the next table was identified as one of the twin daughters of the actor, Jimmy Stewart. Since fame and fortune is always a magnet, even to World Bank fonctionnaires, we spent much of the evening entranced by Kelly's stories of her childhood and father, made even more special by the remnants of the Rana palace environs. For a couple hours, we were happily entwined in the history of the Yak and Yeti and tales of Hollywood, flavoured by the tasty delicacies of the

Nepalese kitchen and the dulcet tones of the unseen musician. A magical evening never forgotten.

<u>Soaltee Hotel</u>

That September 1973 trip, which was also meant to oversee the long-delayed Tourism Project, started on an uncertain note. I decided this time to stay at the Soaltee Hotel, which had been financed by the IFC. The morning after my arrival, I learned that this was the beginning of a six-day religious festival period, meaning all Government offices would be closed for the first week of my visit. I confirmed with my managers in Washington, D.C. that I should stay until I finished my assignment. Thus, six days of no meetings began. By chance that first morning at breakfast, I met Herbert, a Malaysian lawyer from the Asian Development Bank, who was in Kathmandu checking on their projects. Herbert was tall, young and intelligent, and for the remainder of the six-day forced break in our routine, we spent a lot of time together. We walked around much of Kathmandu, ate at various restaurants, and talked of international development from our respective points of view. It was a quiet time which allowed each of us to unwind and get to know each other personally as well as institutionally. Not something that happened often on most Bank missions. Herbert eventually left the Asian Development Bank, and moved to Washington, D.C. He became a member of the legal department of the International Monetary Fund, the Bank's sister institution on 19th Street, and by chance, ended up buying a house in

McLean Estates in northern Virginia, only a hundred yards from where my family and I lived in the same housing development.

From our stay at the Soaltee Hotel, I have retained one vision that I have never forgotten. Eating breakfast next to a large window looking out at a half-acre area of grass, I was surprised to see a row of twenty women on their hands and knees as I glanced outside the window. I noticed that they were dressed in typical Nepalese clothing, which was colourful and attractive. Eventually I focused on what they were doing. This long line of young girls and women were on their knees, using their hands to "cut" grass, one blade at a time. One blade at a time! Forty hands grabbing, ripping the top off the blade, and then grabbing another. It was like a dance. When all twenty had completed "mowing" all the grass in front of them, they each picked up the piece of cloth on which they were kneeling, and in dance-like moves, the whole line moved forward six inches, put down their pieces of cloth, and began the exercise all over again. A human lawnmower. I was shocked enough never to have forgotten my impressions of this scene. Employment being more important than using machines to achieve the same result.

<u>Shopping</u>

One Saturday on this Fall trip, I decided to go shopping on my own. Rather than wandering through the centre of town again, I went outside of the city centre to try to find something different and unique to bring home. I had already bought enough jewellery for a lifetime since the bargain basement prices had remained unchanged during the year I had visited Nepal. The oil price rises in late 1973 had not yet occurred, so anyone trying to start a jewellery store could have done it on a shoestring.

What else would be unusual from Nepal? I visited the Boudhanath Stupa, one of the largest spherical stupas in the world. It was built in the fifth century A.D., by Tibetans as a Buddhist shrine. Many Tibetans traded with Nepal over the centuries and brought their religious practices with them. This Stupa was about seven miles from the city centre. Upon arrival, I was surprised by the size and height of the blinding white Stupa. It was crowned with a four sided, golden coloured, piece of metal which glowed in the sun on top of the bright, white Stupa. Multi-coloured flags decorated the Stupa, attached to long ropes which reached from the top of the Stupa to the buildings which surrounded the Stupa.

I walked around the Stupa a couple times, hypnotized by the prayer wheels which turned in the wind. I discovered that the low buildings which encompassed the Stupa were stores, with owners selling their wares in front. I looked at a myriad of items, totally undecided what to buy. There were trinkets, cloths of amazing colours, religious artifacts, old coins, handicrafts; the total range of bric-a-brac that one finds when visiting a new country. Then one man asked me to enter his not very tall store so he could show me more interesting objects d'art. I stooped down so I could enter the shop and had to remain on my knees when I got inside. It was dark inside and smelled of incense. There were many objects for sale, of a better quality than what one saw displayed on the tables outside. I think he saw that I was hooked, ready to buy something. He opened a low cupboard which he had to crawl into on his hands and knees and brought out a piece of cloth. I had no idea what it was. He showed me an old Tibetan thangka, which pictured an Indian Goddess throwing lightning bolts at the world while astride an orange striped tiger. Very dark brown contrasting with tiger orange, a delightfully painted scene. He said it was seventy years old (he implied that this made it even more valuable) and that because I was such a valuable customer, he would sell it at his best price. I paid fifty dollars for this ancient thangka, one I still have to this day. Whether it was seventy years old or seven days old, I cannot be sure, as there was a proliferation of "ancient" Nepalese coins one could buy in any Kathmandu street. Ancient coins minted down the street hours before.

During one visit to Kathmandu, we decided that we wanted to see the Chinese (Tibet) border to the northeast of the city. A new road was being built to connect the two countries. China was not open to business at that time, so any visit to or near China, evoked a bit of scare-mongering. The drive was beautiful with mountains and lush green valleys everywhere. There was no traffic as the road was still under construction. When we got about two hours out of Kathmandu, we were told by our handlers that we could go no further without specific Chinese Government permission, which none of us had. We got out of the car, took some photos with our cameras (no smart phones then), bundled back into the car and returned over the next two hours to Kathmandu, happy to report that we had been to the "Chinese border", or thereabouts.

Flights of Fancy

Maybe it was the long travel times, maybe it was bad luck or maybe it was merely coincidence. During my two years of travel into and out of Kathmandu, I had a series of experiences which would test any international traveller. On a flight from Calcutta to Kathmandu, we flew on Thai Airways. After about thirty minutes, the captain reported to all that we were turning back to Calcutta since there was a storm in Kathmandu that would make it impossible to land. On return to Calcutta, we were given rooms for the night at the old and well-established Grand Hotel. One passenger and I started to stroll outside the hotel. We had not taken ten steps when we were surrounded by at least a hundred persons, hands out and aggressively begging for money. We turned back and spent the day lolling in the sun by the pool before flying to Kathmandu the next day.

On another flight to Kathmandu, also from Calcutta, we flew on Burma Airways. We were in the usual Bank purchased business class seats. When I looked at the seat configuration in business class and economy class, I saw that both were six seats across. Burmese socialism. The stewardesses were dressed in very colourful Burmese dresses. They served our meal with politeness and a smile. Economy class passengers were served tea and one roll. Business class passengers got tea and two rolls. We all got smiles from the hostesses.

In 1974, at the end of one visit to Kathmandu, I was taken to lunch by Alexander, the Bank's Resident Representative. He was an old Asia hand, and very useful in teaching me about Nepalese culture and specifics about my counterparts in the Government. We had become good friends over the time I was working on projects in Nepal. That lunch he treated me to prawns, not a traditional dish in a Nepalese kitchen. They were tasty and made our meal a medley of food and chat. What they were not was fresh. When I got to Delhi Airport, while waiting for the flight back to Europe later that night, in the endless heat of the evening I suddenly felt ill. Not just ill, violently ill. I spent the next two hours going into and out of the bathroom. All aspects of me were out of control. Horrible vomiting and worse other things. I thought I would never be able to get on the flight, but somehow I felt well enough to fly on Air India. I did not eat on that flight.

Again in 1974, I flew from Kathmandu to Delhi, but this time, just after we took off, a major sandstorm covered all of Delhi. No flight was permitted to land. The RNAC pilot decided to drop us in Lucknow, a city I had never visited before. We arrived around 7 pm, were driven from the airport in buses, and allocated rooms at a local hotel. The heat was intense, even at night, and I remember after an enjoyable evening of drinks with several of the other passengers, a long and sleepless evening in Lucknow. We left for the airport at 7 am the next morning, giving no time to taste the cuisine or purchase any artefacts from this ancient city.

Another flight from Nepal back to London had a different surprise for me. We flew to Delhi, where I was to board an Alitalia flight to Rome, then London. When I got settled into my first-class seat, the Italian man next to me and I started talking. After our meal, he made me an offer. We would flip a coin to see who would sleep on the two soft seats and who would sleep on the floor. I think he used an ancient Nepalese coin, as he won the right to sleep on the seats and I spent the flight back to Rome sleeping on the floor. A first-class lesson for sure. When we got to Rome, it was cloudy, very cloudy. The aircraft attempted to land but even at one hundred feet above the runway, the clouds blocked any view of the runway. The pilot revved up the engine just before we landed, headed back into the sky and told the passengers that the next stop was London, not Rome. Fortunately for me, that was my destination. My seatmate was more than a bit out of joint when he heard we would not land in Rome.

Ajit of the Taj Hotel Group

In 1974, as I left Kathmandu for what was to be my last trip as a member of the Bank, I was asked to fly to Bombay to meet with Ajit, the CEO of the Taj Hotel Group, to ascertain if they were seriously interested in managing the Yak and Yeti Hotel when it was built. Ajit had joined the Taj Hotel Group in 1961 and quickly worked his way up to CEO by the time of my visit. The Taj Hotel Group were traditionally an India-only hotel management group; Nepal would have been the site of their first management contract outside of India, though not that far away, either in kilometres or culture. When I arrived at the hotel, Ajit and his experienced yet young management team treated me to a tour of the Taj Mahal Palace Hotel, its flagship hotel. It was opened in 1903, the first hotel in the Indian Hotel Company Ltd Group, adjacent to the site where the iconic Gateway of India arch would be constructed in 1911 to mark the visit to India of King George V of Britain. Ajit and his efficient and friendly management team used the most modern data management systems available at the time; yet they still valued service above all other objectives in their business. I will always remember our meeting in Ajit's upper floor office, with magnificent views of the city and the ocean, and his humour and graciousness in our brief negotiations. Behind this warm front, he was tough as steel and led the Taj Hotel Group to becoming a major international hotelier in future years.

As it turned out, the Taj Hotel Group never finalized a management agreement for the Yak and Yeti Hotel. There were many reasons for this, not the least of which was the difficulties faced by Taj Hotel Group in dealing with its Nepalese counterparts. Its first overseas hotel under its management was in Sana'a, Yemen (where I, by chance, assisted the Government of Yemen in 2008 in drafting and enacting a new foreign investment law; yes, that too is another story). The Yak and Yeti found other managers after its construction.

Years later, in 1992, a client of mine in Tanzania who wanted to build the first one hundred percent, privately owned and managed hotel in Dar-es-Salaam, joined me on a trip to Bombay.I had arranged for us to meet with Ajit and his very experienced hotel team. Ajit's graciousness never lessened. He was willing to listen to our request to manage a new hotel in Tanzania; they were then managing hotels outside of India. He remembered our earlier discussions in 1974 about the Yak and Yeti Hotel but never regretted his decision not to operate in Nepal. Eventually the Taj Hotel Group decided not to manage my client's hotel in Tanzania, although it was already managing the Pa Modzi Hotel in Lusaka. Through my work in Nepal, I developed a business friendship which lasted many years. A lesson learned over many decades of international business is how important it is to maintain contacts with people you meet in the course of your business travels who are nice to you. Even without the internet, a strong relationship does not die.

Completed: April 30, 2021

ENCHANTMENT WITH MOSCOW

I was descending in a capsule. To a celestial body. Or so it seemed. September 1991. My first trip to Moscow, the heart of the Soviet Union. Home of the Kremlin and colourful, multi-domed Saint Basil's Cathedral. One month after the failed August 19 coup against Soviet President Mikhail Gorbachev.

Based in Washington, D.C., I was a 49-year-old lawyer in a large, international law firm. This was to be my next adventure, added to my quiver of visits to (at that time) 20 African countries. I was with my client, Noli, of Mansons Limited, the developer of a new, privately owned hotel in Dar-es-Salaam, Tanzania. The hotel was to become the largest privately owned company in a country immersed in *ujamaa* socialism, designed, dictated and implemented by President Nyerere. Through the mechanism of a unique debt swap which Noli and I had structured and negotiated with the Trade Representative at the Soviet Embassy in Tanzania, we were invited by the Soviet Ministry of Foreign Economic Relations to come to Moscow to negotiate with the Soviet Government's counterparty for the project, VVO Technoexport. VVO Technoexport was a foreign trade organization (FTO), which was a special type of entity in the Soviet Government structure. FTOs were established under the Ministry of Foreign Economic Relations to facilitate export and import operations in specific branches of the Soviet economy.

A 24-year journey had led me to this fate. Steps along the way included the Peace Corps in Malawi, the Malawi Ministry of External Affairs, the World Bank in Washington, D.C., Citibank in Nairobi, Kenya and three private American law firms, two small and focused on Africa and one gigantic and focused on the US and beyond. I had already lived for five years in Blantyre, Malawi and eight years in Nairobi, Kenya. My only exposure to countries behind the Iron Curtain was during a summer holiday to Europe in 1962 as a student. At that time, I spent a day in East Berlin, crossing into this part of the city through the infamous Checkpoint Charlie. I was open-mouthed; as late as 1962, East Berlin was a bombed-out city with evidence of the war on every block. By chance, a fifteen year old boy I met in the city became my guide for the day, showing me nooks and crannies I would not otherwise have found. I don't remember if I was sad at the sight of the city; I do remember my shock at the destruction which had lasted seventeen years.

The airport where we landed in Moscow, Sheremetyevo, had been constructed anew for the 1980 Olympics, the only Olympic Games which the USA ever boycotted. It was only eleven years later, but I felt like I was walking through an ancient ruin. Each step into this dusky, dusty, dark airport evoked a feeling of apprehension. The ceiling was comprised of a strange field of metal circles into which low wattage bulbs had been inserted. Some even were working. All the passengers were funnelled down two flights of stairs toward six immigration stations. However, to get to one of these stations, each passenger had to go through a gated, wooden entrance, one person at a time. The passengers squeezed and pushed down the stairs toward this single-entry point. If two or more aircraft arrived at the same time, it would take as long as three hours to traverse the stairs, pass through the gate, go through the immigration process and eventually find oneself in the baggage claim area.

The immigration process at each station was an experience. Behind and above each passenger standing before an immigration officer was a mirror, hung so that the immigration officer could see the back of your head as well as your face. If you had a shapka (hat) on, you had to take it off. In those days, the immigration officers did not speak English. And many passengers, such as myself, did not speak Russian. It made for interesting exchanges of information. It took several minutes for each passenger to get an entry stamp in the passport. Almost always your bag was waiting for you, arriving long before immigration had been cleared.

Customs clearance could be fast or slow, depending on what the customs officers felt on the day. That day, we walked without interference through the door into the Soviet Union. We had arrived. Outside we were met by two officials of VVO Technoexport, Dmitry Golaiev and Victor Dashinsky. The mode of transport surprised us; a Chrysler minivan. The last thing I ever expected was to jump into an American car upon arrival in Moscow. The door slid open and we jumped in. We had arrived!!

It was early evening, already dark, as we headed toward the Penta Hotel near Olympiskiy Prospekt. Even in those days, it seemed a long trip, taking about 45 minutes. The highway into the city was not as crowded as I expected. The homes and office buildings were unfamiliar; the street lighting dark and inconsistent. Each mile was a new mile in my life. Each landmark was strange, each intersection unknown. Who could have imagined that I would spend in the future more than ten years of my life being driven on that same highway? How would I then know that this highway would become a familiar entrance into and exit from Moscow for such a long time?

The Penta Hotel is part of the Lufthansa hotel chain. It provided an oasis of Western comfort in an unfamiliar city. More a motel than a luxurious hotel, it was simple, sleek – a warm welcome at the start of our trip. Looking out from the window in my room that evening into the dark night, I could not even imagine what events had taken place in my line of sight over the years.

A happy surprise for me was finding that my former World Bank lawyer colleague and very close friend, Sherif, was also at the Penta Hotel when we arrived. Serendipity? Seeing Sherif in the elevator provided me with a boost of confidence. How could things go wrong when my good friend was sharing the Moscow air with me?

Though tired, I hardly slept. The excitement of the coming day made me restless. A hot shower and a normal breakfast the next morning, served as one would find in any other city, helped settle me down. Coffee and food, normality in this alien city. The restaurant was bright, busy and the day sunny. A premonition?

We were picked up by Dmitry and Victor in the minivan. Our now comfortable and familiar Chrysler minivan. We were whisked off to the VVO Technoexport office on the embankment (naberezhnaya) of the Moscow River, in an eight-story building bulging with Ministry of Foreign Economic Relations related entities. I didn't know it yet, but the building we entered was very "Soviet" in design and appearance, reflecting Soviet office standards throughout Moscow. Wide and dark lonely corridors, high ceilings, wooden walls and parquet floors, and doors announcing in Russian the name of the official who occupied the silent and mysterious office space behind the door.

We took an elevator to the fourth floor and were led into the office of the CEO of VVO Technoexport, Victor Velichko. With a big smile, a warm handshake and greetings in English, Victor welcomed us to Moscow and to VVO Technoexport. Little did I know then that he would become one of my closest friends over the next almost thirty years. As with all CEO offices in Moscow, it was large and full of many chairs and sofas for visitors and an omnipresent photograph of the then Soviet leader. Just as one would find in every African country I had visited, there was a photograph of the Russian President on the wall behind the desk of the head of the office.

After our initial introductions to Victor, we were led into a large conference room to begin the discussions on the draft Memorandum of Understanding which we had forwarded to VVO Technoexport before our arrival. In the conference room were all of the senior officials of VVO Technoexport. They occupied seats around three-fourths of a very long table; Noli and I sat alone on a short side. Two against twenty. All faces were then unfamiliar, but over a period of years, they were to become faces of close friends and colleagues.

This was my first negotiation in the Soviet Union. One aspect was a big surprise, unexpected and did not please me. Almost all of the twenty VVO Technoexport officials smoked cigarettes. One after another. Although the room was a large one, soon a white, pale cloud enveloped the negotiations. For the team from VVO Technoexport, this was normal. For Noli and myself, both non-smokers, it was a difficult environment to work in. Over my next twenty years of living and working in the Soviet Union and Russia, I would have the same experience in even smaller rooms and with thicker clouds of white smoke.

Also provided at every meeting of this type was the standard samovar for making tea along with plates of sweet biscuits and chocolates to nibble on. Moscovites are excellent hosts, whether in their offices or their homes. Food and drink are part of the brotherhood of humankind, and in Moscow, no matter the difficulty of the negotiations or the bitterness between individuals around a table, food and drink is available. Of course, if one wanted coffee or water, these were on the table too. But they could not compete with the elegance and the history of the samovar.

The subject of the negotiation was to arrange for VVO Technoexport to become a shareholder in a legal entity which we were going to establish in Tanzania to design, build and operate a new five-star hotel in Dar-es-Salaam. The reason for Soviet participation in the ownership of the proposed hotel was the result of a debt swap which had been agreed in principle between the Governments of the Soviet Union and Tanzania. In accordance with the inter-governmental agreement, US$36 million of Tanzanian debt to the Soviet Union (only about one-twentieth of the total amount of Tanzania's debt to the Soviet Union) would be converted into Tanzanian shillings, which would be used for the construction of the hotel. As part of the debt swap, the US Dollar amount of these obligations would be written off. For the contribution of these funds to the project, VVO Technoexport was to obtain a sixty percent (60%) shareholding in the new Tanzanian company that would own the hotel. Noli's company, Mansons, would have ten percent (10%) of the shares.

The Memorandum of Understanding on the table was a four-page document which set forth the rights and obligations of each party. Victor Velichko and his colleagues had several comments on and amendments to the draft. Many of their suggestions arose from their lack of experience with more Western business concepts. VVO Technoexport was expert at trading commodities, particularly base metals. But they had no experience or expertise in analyzing the proposed project, the proposed legal structure and the estimated revenues and expenditures which would arise from the operation of the hotel.

At that time, another unfamiliar aspect of our negotiations which became *de rigueur* was the requirement for interpretation from Russian to English and back. An interpreter can make or break a negotiation. It would be uncommon to have simultaneous interpretation at most business negotiations in Moscow. Instead, either each party had its own interpreter or the two parties would agree on an interpreter to serve both sides. At this first negotiation, Noli and I had to rely on the abilities of the interpreter provided by VVO Technoexport. Interpretation is influenced by the length of each speaker's presentation and the ability of the interpreter to understand the nuances of both languages. The former problem can be solved by requiring speakers to speak slowly and make statements of no more than a couple sentences at a time. The latter problem cannot be overcome if the interpreter isn't colloquially competent in both languages. This can have a positive or deleterious effect on the outcome of negotiations.

Nevertheless, within a couple hours we agreed on changes to the draft Memorandum. The VVO Technoexport team asked how we proposed to make the changes. I requested them to give me no more than an hour, first to change the draft in the computer which I had brought with me and then to print the updated draft for further consideration. While everyone waited around the table, smoking as if there was no tomorrow and drinking the ubiquitous tea and coffee, it took me a short time to make the proposed changes on my computer. When I opened the printer and hooked it up with the computer, the VVO Technoexport team was aghast. They had never seen such equipment. This was state of the art at the time, but the state wasn't that artful. It took many minutes to print each page. At the end of forty-five minutes, we had the updated draft ready to be scrutinized by the parties. Victor Velichko told me some years later that VVO Technoexport should have gone immediately into the computer business. It would have made the company and the employees quite wealthy.

On our way back to the hotel, we drove along Gorky Street, the Fifth Avenue or the Oxford Street of Moscow. It was late afternoon, already the sun having disappeared and what should have been a flourishing market street was not to be found. All the stores on Gorky Street had closed by this time. Many had virtually nothing in the windows, their wares nowhere seen. What should have been a well-lit thoroughfare was in fact more like a dark and quiet alley. The lights either didn't work or had little power to show themselves. It felt as we had been taken back in time to a period when lights didn't exist and days ended when sundown was reached.

It didn't take long for this situation to change. Gorky Street has been given its old mantle, re-named Tverskaya Street. The world's fanciest stores are all present there.

Windows are filled with the latest fashions and gizmos. And the lights glitter all night. A commercial revolution has taken place.

Negotiations having ended with both sides pleased, Noli and I decided to visit the Kremlin the next day. Even the word "Kremlin" was ominous. It signified power, unknown and unmitigated power. Hard power. The power of inter-continental ballistic missiles, of unexploded nuclear bombs, of MiG jets screaming overhead, of tanks speeding on the ground, of the sounds of the steps of millions of soldiers marching in unison. The Kremlin, where the dark arts were forged and practiced; where the footsteps of Lenin and Stalin, Khrushchev and Brezhnev, and more recently Gorbachev could be heard and felt. Familiar Soviet names with unfamiliar ways of making decisions that affected even the small, suburban town outside Chicago where I grew up.

On our way to the Kremlin, we first went to the GUM, the State Universal Magazine (store). This three storied building is almost 800 feet long, and features a glass domed roof built in the late 19th century. Our visit was as disappointing as our Gorky Street tour had been. We traversed all three floors of the GUM. Again, an absence of goods was everywhere. In one store we entered, they had just received thousands of cans of Angolan sardines. So, at least there were some rows of shelves filled with these tasty morsels. Nothing more was offered in this store. And equivalent emptiness was offered on all three floors. It was 1991, and this was the state of commerce in the Soviet Union at that time.

After the fall of the Soviet Union and the privatization of the GUM, the building later became a fancy shopping mall, with familiar world-class names displayed on each of the three tiers. Coffee shops and restaurants, modern and well appointed, with loud and upbeat rap music, replaced the staid elegance of the old GUM. And it is not alone. Today, there are dozens and dozens of similar, more modern and some even larger shopping malls all over Moscow and Russia.

Next, we walked into Red Square, where the May 1st rallies and military parades take place each year, always presided over by the leaders of the day. Now that the Communists are no longer in power, the so-called elected officials who run the country proudly stand on the dais and watch the tanks roll by, the planes fly by and the men march by. Red Square is made up of an endless number of thick, gray, brick-shaped stones. Many people, famous and otherwise, have trod those stones over the centuries; now we are among them.

We then drove around to the entrance to the Kremlin. We walked into the Taynitsky Garden which is an urban park open to the public and located within the walls of the Kremlin. The park is named after the Taynitskaya Tower in the Kremlin Wall; the entire Kremlin being a UNESCO World Heritage Site. The word Kremlin means citadel in Russian. There are many scattered throughout the Soviet Union. The best known is the one in Moscow. It consists of five palaces, four cathedrals, the Wall surrounding the Kremlin and various towers spaced in the Wall. The Tsar's former Moscow residence is there, called the Grand Kremlin Palace. During Khruschev's regime, the immense Palace of Congresses was built on the Kremlin grounds. In this building were held the Congresses of the Communist Party of the Soviet Union. I later attended concerts and ballet performances in its massive six thousand seat theatre.

Walking in the park on that sunny, languid afternoon, Noli and I wandered into and out of various churches and palaces, particularly impressed by the icons in the churches. We also enjoyed the flowers of late autumn, the trim green lawn, a lonely statue of Lenin which stood in a remote area of the garden and most of all, the Tsar Bell, the world's largest bell. Manufactured in the mid-18th century, the Bell, which is twenty feet high and with a circumference of twenty feet, has a large crack, which resulted from cold water being poured on the Bell to put out a fire which raged in the wooden frame holding the Bell before it was removed from its construction site. Consequently, the Bell has never rung, yet sits proudly in the Kremlin garden, an attraction marvelled at by both foreign and Russian visitors alike. Noli and I took many photos of this enormous human effort, whose function was never achieved.

On that afternoon, we were far from our families, far from our usual lives and homes. Yet we were in a place where there was quiet and peace as we walked in the soft, afternoon September sun, which felt familiar and comforting on one hand and yet so alien on the other. A quiet interlude at the end of a business negotiation, while at the same time, standing near the spiritual heartbeat of an as yet unknown country.

Completed: July 8, 2020

Printed in Dunstable, United Kingdom

66676935R00137